LO *and* BEHOLD!

LO *and* BEHOLD!

The power of
Old Testament storytelling

TREVOR DENNIS

First published in Great Britain in 1991

Society for Promoting Christian Knowledge
36 Causton Street
London SW1P 4ST
www.spckpublishing.co.uk

Reprinted once
Reissued 2010

British Library Cataloguing-in-Publication Data
A catalogue record for this book is available from the British Library

ISBN 978–0–281–06373–4

1 3 5 7 9 10 8 6 4 2

Printed in Great Britain by Ashford Colour Press

Produced on paper from sustainable forests

CONTENTS

For Caroline,
Eleanor, Sarah,
Joanna, and Timothy,
without whose love
I would not have written
this book

PREFACE

This book aims to give readers unfamiliar with the Old Testament a glimpse of the wealth of material to be discovered there, and whet their appetite for more, and to encourage those with some study behind them to go deeper into the text and ask new questions.

It does not attempt to be anything approaching a comprehensive treatment of the storytelling of the Old Testament. Its method, as explained in the Introduction, has demanded the selection of a very few narratives for detailed discussion, and while it ranges at times far and wide outside those texts, some of the finest examples of the Hebrew storyteller's art have been passed by. Sometimes, as in the case of the David stories, such material has been neglected (with much regret on the author's part), even though it belongs to the larger narrative with which most of the book is concerned.

It does not demand any prior knowledge from the reader, and care has been taken to avoid technical terms (the only one the author has himself spotted is 'theophany', meaning, 'appearance of God', but then the word has such a bright ring about it, and 'appearance of God' is so cumbersome and dull by comparison!).

It will be of use, we hope, to a great variety of people: to lay men and women who simply wish to get deeper into their scriptures, to those in training to be Readers or Lay Preachers, to ordinands, to theology undergraduates, and to clergy or lay theology graduates brought up on the historical critical approach to the Bible and wanting something more.

It seeks to make original contibutions to scholarship, in its handling of the detail of particular passages, in the connections it makes between one passage and another, and in its exposition of the shape and development of the long narrative that winds its way from Genesis to Kings (we would argue that that material clamours to be read as a single work, despite the fact that generally it is still firmly split into Pentateuch and Deuteronomistic History, or Torah and Former Prophets). Therefore, while it has been written primarily with a readership outside academia in mind, it might, I would also hope, be of interest to biblical scholars.

In these days, when at last, thank God!, Jews and Christians are beginning to read each other's books, it may be that some Jews will pick up this one, which after all is concerned with documents which were their scriptures long before the Church got hold of them. If they not only pick it up but read it, and are not put off by its occasional references to the New Testament and specifically Christian beliefs, and its espousal of those beliefs, they will discover that the author is as much in love with the Hebrew Bible as they are.

Though written with what we trust is a proper academic rigour, it is aimed at the enriching of faith (not necessarily, as our last paragraph may indicate, of Christian faith). Thus it attempts to bridge the gulf commonly fixed between academic and devotional studies.

Trevor Dennis
Salisbury
June 1990

ACKNOWLEDGEMENTS

I wrote this book during a sabbatical allowed me for the purpose by the Governors of Salisbury and Wells Theological College. To them I am very grateful. I owe an even larger debt of gratitude to the staff and students of the College, not only to those currently among its members, but also to those who have been my colleagues and friends these past eight years. I have always found the College an immensely stimulating place. From my colleagues on the staff I have received a very great deal of friendship and encouragement, and they have been remarkably patient with my frequent expressions of enthusiasm for my subject. As for the students, they have continually showed me new things in the text, and have sometimes changed my reading of it radically. Without their commitment to the task of interpretation, their willingness to engage with the text and let it do its work, and the enthusiasm they themselves have so often developed for the material we have been studying together, I would not have so thoroughly enjoyed my work, and this book would probably never have been written.

Undoubtedly, however, and inevitably, it is to the members of my immediate family, who somehow manage to live with me every day, that I owe the greatest debt. To them this book is dedicated.

INTRODUCTION

Imagine a king in a great palace with two rooms packed with treasure. The door of one of the rooms is constantly being opened as the king and his courtiers bring out items for display. The treasures of that room are treated with reverence, sometimes with great ceremony, often with love. Every item is examined in detail, and the pedestals on which they are put for all to admire are very high. The door of the other room, however, is for the most part kept locked. Though it is the larger of the two rooms, packed with a far greater number of fine things than the other, it is rarely entered. Sometimes some of its treasures are brought out into the state or private rooms of the palace for display. But then often they are put on low tables in corners where few take notice of them. There are some exceptionally fine things among them, as those at the court recall from time to time. But the general opinion is that the treasures from that room are poor, dull things, perhaps even ugly things, compared to the bright treasures of the other room.

For the past eight years I have taught the Old Testament in an English theological college. Increasingly I have become aware of how unfamiliar the younger students are with the Old Testament when they arrive. To many of them it is literally a closed book. I cannot safely assume any knowledge of it at all, even of what I would have guessed before were the 'better known' passages. Rarely have they heard it read in church. Even more rarely have they heard it preached on. When they have heard it referred to, it has usually been in words of disparagement. It has been written off as inculcating legalism and revealing a vindictive God, or else as outmoded and proved by modern science to be misguided. At best it has been seen as coming a poor second to the truly Christian scriptures of the Church, the New Testament.

Even among the older students, those in their thirties, forties and fifties, those brought up on a diet of Mattins and Evensong with long lessons from the Old Testament, many have succumbed to the fashion of the day. As they approach the Old Testament course they expect to find it boring and beside the point, or worse. They do not tell me that at the start. They admit it somewhat sheepishy when the course is finished and their eyes have opened to the treasures they have been neglecting for so long.

I do not blame the students, but I am alarmed by them. After all, they are in training for the ordained ministry of the Church and are among its most deeply committed members. If the Old Testament is closed to them, to whom is it open? It may well be that there are other denominations in Britain, or Churches in other parts of the world, where Christians act as householders who bring out of their treasure what is new and old in equal measure (to quote the New Testament!), but I must speak of what I know.

The fault lies partly with Old Testament scholarship. For many decades now it has been largely preoccupied with looking through the text to what may or may not lie behind it. Scholars have come to the text as a window, and from their study desks have peered through it trying to make out the details of the historical events, the cultural and social conditions, the ritual, the processes of composition that lie on the other side of it. 'It still seems to most scholars in the field much more urgent to inquire, say, how a particular psalm might have been used in a hypothetically reconstructed temple ritual than how it works as an achieved piece of poetry.' That was Robert Alter, a distinguished American scholar, writing in 1980. Things are changing now, but have not yet changed.

The results of this historical approach have often proved immensely illuminating, and for very many they have awakened an interest in the text and brought it alive. I was reared on it myself and it did that for me. At times we will be appealing directly to it in this book. Undoubtedly, however, it has severe limitations. It can lead us into dark labyrinths of argument and questions of immense complexity that leave all but the experts floundering. The non-experts can begin to weigh up the arguments, but have little or no chance of making any original contributions to the debate. It is intellectually élitist. Secondly it demands a certain detachment from the text. This has enabled Biblical Studies to retain a certain respectability in modern secular universities, but it is a serious drawback for those Christians who would wish to approach the text as the possible if not probable vehicle of the word of God, or for those who would wish simply to enjoy reading it. Often it comes to the text with questions which only scholars tend to ask. Sometimes those outside academia hear of the questions and think they ought to be asking them too, but give up because they cannot hope to supply any answers. They are left feeling guilty or inadequate, or else defensive of their 'uninformed position'.

Exciting things are happening, however. Since the mid-seventies, with a few trail-blazers before that, many books have appeared which have approached the text not as a window but as a picture. They have been concerned to look *at* the text, at what it says and how it says it. They have encouraged not a detachment from the text, but an engagement with it, an enjoyment of it. The exercise of interpretation they have promoted has not been an entirely cerebral one. It has brought the imagination into play, and the emotions. It has wished for people, whether Christians or Jews or otherwise, to be caught up in the material, to be excited by it, amused by it, disturbed by it. It has been encouraging readers to allow the text to have its way with them. It has asked them to *pay attention* to the text, notice things they have not noticed before, feel things about it they have not felt before.

It has asked them to pay great respect to the integrity of the text. Such harm is done in the Church and beyond by people using the Bible for their own ends, making it serve their own sometimes sinister and destructive purposes. Some use it to hound homosexuals or to keep women from positions of power, some to crush tribal cultures and swamp them with Western capitalism, or even to enable the more nefarious activities of the CIA. The approach of which I am speaking demands by contrast that people come to the text with fresh minds, and expects that they will be surprised by it and often made to feel uncomfortable. Such expectations are based on the astonishing nature of the text itself, and on the God who has spoken to so many through it, a God who is himself so full of surprises, and so distrubing of our prejudices, pride and complacency, and our fear.

One great advantage of the approach is that it does not demand an enormous amount of background knowledge before we begin. The 'ordinary' reader can have a go, and can come up with original and illuminating comment. More's the pity then, at least for those of us in Britain, that most of the recent books making use of it have appeared in America and have reached a small, almost exclusively academic audience over here. Some have been written and published in Britain, but these have been largely designed for that same academic readership. Things are changing, however; the good news is beginning to be preached to a larger congregation. This book has been written in a desire to assist that process in some small way and to accelerate it.

Our method will be to select a few stories and go through each in detail. With the exception of Genesis 1, which comes so close to being a poem, all the poetry of the Old Testament will be neglected in the process. The books of the prophets, the Book of Psalms, and the Wisdom literature, Proverbs, Job, and Ecclesiastes will not be covered. They and other great treasures will be left locked away. But many find poetry more daunting than stories. For those bravely prepared to become enchanted by the Old Testament, its stories provide the best way in.

Some of our stories are well known amongst those who are familiar with the Old Testament at all, and are the subject of frequent debate. Others have received relatively little attention. Some of them are found inspiring by many, others are commonly regarded as obscure, difficult, even as deeply disquieting.

Each of the first six chapters of this book deals with just two passages in detail, and the seventh with only one, though that is a complete work. We have quite deliberately kept the list of passages short, for that will enable us to begin to pay the text the close attention it deserves. But in truth far more material will be covered than that contained in the thirteen stories. With the exception of Jonah we will need to consider the places the chosen stories occupy in the larger narrative to which they belong. That will mean paying heed not merely to the stories that immediately precede them or come hard on their heels, but to material widely separated from them, and to the thrust of the whole great story that winds its tortuous way from Genesis to Kings. We will find ourselves making connections between one story and another, discovering echoes that often the storytellers clearly intended us to hear. In various ways each of our chapters will lead into the next.

We do not hope to give definitive readings of the text. We would, indeed, deny that there are any such things. We will be trying only to give the results of our own dialogue with the material, hoping that others, having learned how to pay closer attention to it themselves, might be stimulated to engage in their own dialogues with it and come up with their own responses.

We will not be attempting to make clear the 'message' of the text. We will be dealing with stories, and stories cannot be reduced to 'messages'. Those who have tried, for example, to reduce the parables of Jesus to messages have invariably come up with something disappointing, and have always been open to the question, 'If that's what Jesus was trying to say, why didn't he say it?' Rather than reduce the stories to anything, we will be hoping to enlarge them and open them up. We will be wishing to make them accessible, so that others might step with us inside the worlds they create and there find themselves changed.

We will begin with Genesis and stay with Genesis till the end of chapter 3. We do not apologize for that. Not only does that book contain many of the most remarkable stories in the whole Bible, but it also sets the scene for all that follows. Its stories are not about the people of God. They are about the planet, indeed the universe, about humankind, and about a few generations of a particular family. The members of that family do become the ancestors of the Israelite people, but the tales of their deeds, of their courage and their fear, their laughter and their anguish, their jealousies and their strong love, have a universality about them which is clear to all who read them with care.

Only when we get beyond Genesis, however, to the giving of the torah as described in Exodus — Deuteronomy, do we reach the very heart of the Old Testament's gospel. Our fourth chapter will cover a good deal of ground in the desert land of Exodus and Numbers in particular, and by the end of it we will be in a better position to understand what 'torah' means, and to appreciate how misleading it is to call it 'the law'.

From Genesis 12 onwards the narrative looks forward to the Israelites' entry into Canaan, and to their becoming an independent people there. Chapter 5 will concern itself with two stories relating to the period of conquest, and the next chapter will give us a glimpse of life under the Israelite kings. By this time we will have come a long way from the bright visions of Genesis 1 and 2 with which we began. The little book of Jonah, sitting apart from the Genesis—Kings narrative, echoing it in several places, making its own amusing and disturbing comment upon it, will in some ways bring us back to the beginning. It is one of the most brilliantly told stories in all Scripture, and one of the most profound. It is very hard to follow, and recognizing that, we will stop once we reach the end of its final scene. We will thus end not with a conclusion, but with a question, for that is how Jonah finishes. That will be appropriate in an enterprise that is meant to whet the appetite, to encourage us to return with further questions to the passages already covered, and to venture out with a new sense of excitement into the equally extraordinary territory beyond them.

We will need to approach our stories not only with an open mind, but with an open Bible. To read the set passages before starting each chapter would be helpful. To look them up continually as we make our way through them will be vital. Almost any version will do, though we have used the RSV as our working translation, and the vast majority of quotations of the text are taken from that, sometimes with small alterations to bring them closer to the original Hebrew.

By the time God's final question to Jonah is reached we wish to have given a glimpse of what a treasure store the Old Testament is.

1

THE WORLD OF GOD'S MAKING

(Genesis 1—3)

We begin, as the Old Testament begins, with two stories of creation, each quite different from the other, possibly centuries apart in their initial composition, but put together by the compiler or author of Genesis to strike sparks from one another.

Each is more than a story of creation. Each is concerned as much with the End as with the Beginning. Each gives a vision not of the world as it is, though, thank God, many of the details are still recognizable and familiar to us, but of the world of God's making, the world that he intends, the world that belongs to his Ending. These creation stories are usually read as stories of the remote past. They are really stories of the present, helping us to put our world into perspective, and they are stories of the future, for when God's purposes are fulfilled, the world *will* be of God's making, not ours.

The good order of Genesis 1

To begin to read Genesis 1 in the original Hebrew is to become aware at once of the beauty, the solemnity of the language, and its poetic quality. It hovers on the border between prose and poetry. That border is never very sharply defined in biblical Hebrew, but at times we can say that the text of this chapter slips over into poetry. It is sonorous speech, hiding its profundity in great simplicity, as all the greatest writing does. Above all it is orderly speech, expressing in its rhythms and repetitions the orderliness of the creation it describes.

God begins here not with nothing, but with fearful and awesome chaos. The earth is there, but it is empty, an utterly lifeless waste, a place where no life can possibly exist unless God transforms it into something quite different. The beginning of verse 2 makes us think of a desert, but the picture immediately shifts to that of a vast mass of water swaying in the pitch blackness. Over this the Spirit of God hovers like a bird, waiting to strike and take chaos for its prey. That is one way of interpreting the Hebrew. Another is to see the mass of water shaken by the wind of God. The Hebrew is ambiguous and we should respect its elusiveness. When dealing with poetic prose such as this, it is not necessary or even proper to choose one possible interpretation and reject another. The text will carry both, and will allow both pictures to enter our imagination.

The first act of God is to speak. 'Let there be light!' He does not address the chaos. Such chaos as this cannot be addressed. The word can only be spoken into the dark. But it is not an empty cry in the wasteland. It is a word charged with the power to create, to transform, to order. The darkness is not banished altogether. It is put in its place. It is put beside God's new creature, light, and given the name 'Night'. God did not create the darkness. It is outside his making. Left to itself it is sinister, and when God looks at the light he has made and declares it fine and beautiful (for that is what the Hebrew word for 'good' means), he does not include the darkness in his delight. Here is the merest hint in the text that this darkness retains the power to become sinister again, to return to being the black dark of the wasteland. Certainly the waters of chaos, divided between those beneath and those above God's new firmament, will take up their old powers of destruction in the story of the Flood. But the talk is not yet of destruction. Nor is it of struggle. This God is not battling with the forces of chaos, winning a victory that is not wholly won. There is none of that at all. Instead the darkness, at the breathing of God's word, ceases to be sinister, and the waters cease to be chaos. They are part now of God's new, emerging order, assigned their places and their functions. Darkness becomes night, and the waters become either the great reservoir above the roof of the sky (so the ancient Israelites envisaged it) which will provide the rain, or else the seas of the earth. God sees what he has done, and it is beautiful. He does not clap his hands in delight. The writer of Genesis 1 is too restrained to picture God doing such a thing, but if our minds do that for us, we will not be far astray.

With the waters in their places the dry land appears and receives its name, 'Earth', its God-given identity. At once, with another word of God spoken, this earth becomes alive with plants and vegetation, each plant carrying within it its own powers of increase and renewal. The deadness of the chaos with which God began is now gone, and God delights again in what he sees.

Day and Night are already in existence. Only now, on the fourth day of creation, are the sun, the moon and the stars created. This seems strange to us, knowing as we do where our light comes from. But the writer of Genesis 1 means to put the heavenly bodies in their place in more senses than one. Almost certainly the passage was first written in Babylonia, during the sixth-century period of exile. The Ancient Near East, like all other parts of the world, was full of creation stories. It was full too of worship of the sun, the moon and the stars. These were thought of as gods, controlling the lives and destinies of creatures on earth. The most famous of the Babylonian creation stories to have survived, *Enuma Elish*, has no description of the creation of the sun and stars. They already exist in that account, and the god Marduk can only assign them to their stations and give them freedom to move across the sky.

Genesis 1 by contrast leaves us in no doubt that all the heavenly bodies are creatures of the one God's creating. Light itself was there mysteriously before them. They did not create light. God did that, and they are there to do his bidding and to administer the giving of light over the earth according to his already well-established pattern. Thus, in the space of five verses, the writer of Genesis 1 takes the rug from under the feet of the ancient so-called science of astrology, and gives calm reassurance to those whose hopes and fears are bound up, even in our own sophisticated world, with the movements of planets and stars. No wonder God sees what he has done and claps his hands again in delight!

More words are then spoken by the creator, charged now with power to fill the waters upon the earth with fish and crocodiles, and the skies with a multitude of species of birds. New words, not heard before, are needed here. The plants had the power of renewal within their seed. The fish and the birds, however, must be given their powers of reproduction in a second act of their creation. So for the first time God addresses creatures of his directly, and he does so with words of blessing: 'God blessed them, saying, "Be fruitful and multiply . . ." ' The first words creatures of God hear are words not of demand, not of judgement, but of blessing. The writer of Genesis 1 understands the grace of God and its priority. Things are not created out of nothing here. They are created out of grace.

Creatures from the heart of God's deliberating

With the next, the sixth day of God's creating, we reach the initial climax of this account. First, as God's word again escapes his lips, the land animals are brought forth from mother Earth (there is a faint echo of the old mythology here), both wild and domestic, and those reptiles that creep upon the ground. The snake in Genesis 3, in the sequel to the second creation story, is condemned to a life of sliding on its belly. For the writer of Genesis 1 there is nothing wrong with creeping. That is what the reptiles were made to do, and God declares them beautiful with the rest.

He does not bless them, however. At least, no words of blessing are expressed at this point. Here is a case where we must be careful not to argue too much from the writer's silence. There are three acts of blessing in this first account of creation, in 1.22, in 1.28, and in 2.3. In the first two cases the blessing confers powers of reproduction and increase. Clearly the writer would not have us believe that those powers were denied to the land animals. Either the blessing is to be taken for granted, or else we must understand the first words of blessing addressed to human beings as covering the animals also.

Whichever option we choose, we see the writer hurrying on to the creation of man and woman. Once there he slows the pace of his account right down, and clothes his language in the most solemn attire he can find. 'Let us make man,' says God, not because suddenly he is plural or conceived as a Trinity, but because the writer uses what the Hebrew grammarians call 'a plural of deliberation'. 'Let us make man in our image, after our likeness,' says God, and upon these words whole books have been built from the early days of Christian doctrine onwards.

Often the books have taken the words out of their context, and have been preocupied with discovering the whereabouts of this 'image and likeness of God' within human nature, or with wondering where it has got to. We need not be surprised by that. The words of verse 27 in particular, where talk of human beings created in the image of God is repeated, have the same quality of simplicity as 'To be, or not to be: that is the question', and like Hamlet's line, are rather wont to rattle round our minds, feeding our imaginations. Unlike Shakespeare's words, however, they are mysterious. We know what Hamlet means. The meaning of these words of Genesis is elusive. That is part of their power and why so much has been written about them. For centuries theologians have been trying to pin them down, or else have used them to support their own prior understanding of human nature.

Put back in their context they are saying something not about human nature but about God's creating. The light, the firmament and the waters above it, the seas, the dry land, the plants, the heavenly bodies, the fish, the crocodiles, the birds and all the land animals have all come into being as a result of God's speaking, God's making, God's dividing. But nothing has been said of where God got the ideas from. In the case of the human beings the act of creation is different. The idea for this creation comes from God himself. He himself is the pattern after which men and women are made. They come from the heart of his deliberating: the Hebrew plural of deliberation makes that clear also.

It is difficult to say more than that without going beyond the hints the text gives us. But the results of God's creating are clear enough: a creature made not to be a slave and skivvy to the gods as in the Babylonian stories, but to rule the earth as God rules creation. Dominion belongs to these human beings, not as of right, not as of their own taking or making, but as a gift from God. Their ruling the earth thus demonstrates God's generosity. God has put the creation in good order. Now human beings must see that that order is kept. The kangaroos, to lapse into a flippancy that is markedly absent from Genesis 1, must not be allowed to get out of hand! The words of Genesis are dangerous ones to hear in a world where human arrogance stands so tall and where technology enables man (usually it is *man*, not woman) to do such harm to the environment. But there is no hint of tyranny in the sovereignty of God pictured in Genesis 1, and there can be nothing tyrannical about the dominion granted to the creature made in his image.

Curiously enough this is substantiated by God's talk about food. He gives the human beings and the animals and birds plants and fruit to eat, but nothing else. There is no mention of meat anywhere. Here is a vision of a world where no creature's survival depends on the killing of another. There are no predators. None are prey. All live on that which contains within itself its own powers of regeneration. This world God sees, and declares very beautiful.

A world familiar yet strange

The work of creation is done, but the account is not finished. It is still to reach its second and final climax. It does not end until 2.4a and by then it has spoken of God's rest, and of his third act of blessing. Other creation stories spoke of God resting at the end. The Babylonian myths did, but with them the rest was very different: it was the leisure of gods who took no further part in things, who created the world and then withdrew. Among all creation stories only Genesis speaks of a day of rest, and a day made blessed and holy. This is not withdrawal, but the setting of rest and holy time within the rhythm of the world's passing. The word 'sabbath' does not occur in the text, but in the Hebrew the words for 'seventh' and 'rested' sound very like it, and are from the same root. There is a play on words here, impossible to reproduce in translation, which would make anyone hearing or reading it immediately think of the sabbath. Thus each sabbath, each seventh day, is declared blessed time, holy time, time set apart for the purposes of God (for that is what holy means in the Old Testament). To step inside its boundaries is to find oneself in God's time, enjoying God's rest. That is the vision here. To observe it is to keep to the rhythms of creation. It is as natural as can be, and far away from the pinched, burdensome thing that Christians have sometimes made it. In my experience Jews understand it better and find it easier to observe in the proper spirit.

The words about the seventh day link the world of Genesis 1 with our own. But the words just before them, about a vegetarian diet for humanity and all the animals, divorce us from the vision. However many people are vegetarian, they will not persuade the thrush to stop bashing snails to bits on the garden path, or get the lion to eat grass. There lies the tension in Genesis 1, and it is part of its great profundity. It presents a vision of a world familiar yet strange to us. We know the astonishing beauty which God so much applauds, yet not all is beautiful. We cannot look at *everything* and declare it 'very good'. Out of chaos God in Genesis 1 puts everything into good order. We have a clearer understanding than the writer of the intricacies and remarkable orderliness of the universe and of what we call the natural world. Yet we see so much disorder too.

The undisturbed beauty and orderliness of the world of Genesis 1 puts into sharper focus the beauty and the ugliness, the order and disorder of the world we know. The world of Genesis 1 is of God's making. The world we know, the world of this planet at least, is also of our making. There is the difference. That is why Genesis 1 speaks most powerfully not of the past but of God's future when

the wolf shall dwell with the lamb,
and the leopard shall lie down with the kid,
and the calf and the lion and the fatling together,
and a little child shall lead them . . .
and the lion shall eat straw like the ox.

(Isa. 11.6,7)

On any reckoning Genesis 1 is a most remarkable story of creation, and one of its most extraordinary features is not in its text at all, but lies with the time it was written. It belongs, as we have said already, to the period of the exile in Babylonia. That means it belongs to the time when the Israelites had suffered the greatest catastrophe of their history, a catastrophe which it would have been quite natural to interpret in terms of the defeat of their God at the hands of the gods of the Babylonians. Jerusalem had been devastated, God's temple destroyed. All had collapsed into disorder; national life was in chaos. The contrast between the world in which the writer lived and the world of his great vision could hardly be greater. His words represent an astonishing declaration of faith, as good as any creed, if not better. They declare that the past, and more importantly the present and the future, belong to God. They are meant in their calm, solemn way to raise hopes as high as heaven. When we move through much darker places in the Old Testament we must bear in our minds how it all began, in this beginning when God created the heavens and the earth. We must not let the vision fade.

Genesis 2 – 3: Exposing the foundations

The second creation story follows hard on the heels of the first. Its focus is much narrower. Creation stories are universal, belonging to all cultures and every part of the world. They fall into two basic categories, those concerned with the creation of the whole world, and those confining themselves to the creation of a particular species. Genesis 1 belongs to the first category, Genesis 2 to the second. Genesis 1 would be impossible to put on stage. Genesis 2 would be perfectly feasible. Its scenes are small and intimate. For the most part only two or three characters are on stage at any one time.

To step out of Genesis 1 into the creation story of Genesis 2 is like coming out of a grand ornate church, filled with incense and the sound of a great organ playing a Bach fugue, into a spring meadow on a fresh, bright sunny morning. This is storytelling. Genesis 1, strictly speaking, was not. That moved to two climaxes, but it cannot be said that it had a plot or drama to it. It was a solemn declaration of faith. Now we find drama in plenty, movement, development, suspense, tension, problems awaiting resolution. It is a brilliant piece of writing, and it is no wonder that it has caught and held the imaginations of so many over the centuries.

Everyone knows the story. Or they think they do. It is at once the best known and the worst known of all the stories in the Old Testament. What most people know is not the text, but the vast structure of doctrine which past theologians have built upon it. The story lies hidden in the foundations and all we see is the building above it. In order to reach this story again, in to enable it to become for us a platform for the *fresh*-spoken word of God, we must first demolish the building, or, at least, move it to another site.

The story is not about Satan or the origin of evil. It is not about the Fall. It is not about original sin. It is not about the root of human wickedness. It does not attempt to take us to the heart of humanity's rotten core. It does not describe how death came into the world. It does not present the female of the species as a wicked temptress. It does not suggest there is something basically wrong with sexual desire. Whatever the merits of the doctrines built upon the story, and most of them are not a patch on the story itself, they do not arise naturally from the text. Their true origins lie elsewhere, often in philosophies which, for all the truth that may lie within them, have little to do with anything in the Bible.

A divine kiss of life, and loneliness answered

Though we have referred to Genesis 2 (by which we mean 2.4b–25) as a creation story, it is clearly much more than that. Only verses 4b–7, 19, and 21–2 are concerned with acts of creation, and the narrative as a whole is linked so intimately with another in 3.1–24 that the two are now a unity. One recent American commentator, Phyllis Trible, has called Genesis 2–3 a love story – 'a love story gone awry' – and that is perhaps a more accurate designation.

It starts with creation well enough, the making of a man. Genesis 1.26–7 described the creation of humankind. As Gregory of Nyssa realized long ago (he was a bishop and theologian of the fourth century CE) all humanity is caught up in that act of creation. Genesis

2.7 speaks of a single individual. This man belongs to the past and to the present and future. He belongs to the past, for the succeeding chapters of Genesis will trace the descent of all human beings back to him. He belongs to the present because his name is simply 'Man'. The word *'adam* in Hebrew means 'man', and indeed it should be translated 'man' throughout Genesis 2 and 3. Nowhere, if we follow the best textual critics, does it appear as the proper name Adam, and many of our versions have to be ignored on the point. The woman also, created later from his rib, is simply 'Woman'. She is not Eve until she is so named by the man at the end. So this story is not just about a couple in the remote past. It is about Man and Woman. It is about us. And this Man and Woman belong to the future also, not because we are given a picture of humanity in all the perfection to which we are called, but because the story shows us how life with God might be lived, and will be when once again the world becomes his Garden.

The acts of creation described in 2.7 and 21–22 are very intimate ones. In the man's case God takes dust from the ground (or from the *'adamah* in Hebrew: another play on words we cannot reproduce), mixes it with water perhaps (if that is why the stream of water is mentioned in verse 6), and with his own hands moulds his body, then kneels over him to give him a divine kiss of life. In the second act God becomes the surgeon, taking a rib from the unconscious man, and then, as only the divine craftsman can, he makes that into a woman. This is the intimacy with God by which and for which human beings are made!

After creating the man God turns to gardening or horticulture and plants a garden for him. Here he has all the food he needs. As in Genesis 1 there is no mention of meat or hunting or killing. The man need only reach up and pick what he requires. It is all too easy, as we will see again when the serpent comes on the scene.

The garden has an ample water supply also. The ancient Israelites lived in a land and at a time when supplies of fresh water could not be taken for granted. In Eden the supply is enough to water the whole earth.

At this point the writer steps aside from his story to give us a short geography lesson. Here is something strange. Eden is a timeless place, a placeless place, somewhere that cannot be pinned down. It belongs somewhere in the east, that is all we are told. It is of God's planting, and it is, as we shall discover, the place where he can be found walking in the cool of the day. It contains two mysterious trees which clearly do not belong to our world but to God's. By the end of Genesis 3 it has passed beyond the sphere of human knowledge for ever. It is not surprising, therefore, to learn that two of the four rivers that flow from it, the Pishon and the Gihon, are not heard of anywhere else. They are shrouded aptly enough in Eden's mystery. But the other two rivers are the Tigris and the Euphrates, the two great rivers of Mesopotamia, which rise in Turkey and flow through Iraq into the Persian Gulf. Suddenly, strangely, we are in the world we know. It is another reminder that this story concerns ourselves. It is about us, and we will find plenty more in it that is familiar.

The Garden of Eden is often pictured as a place of blissful ease, where all manner of things once were well. That also is something we must clear out of the way in order to reach the story.

The newly created man has a place where he belongs, right enough, and all the food and water he needs. Nothing has yet spoiled the naturalness and intimacy of his relations with God. He has the freedom of the place and only one thing is prohibited, the eating of the fruit of the tree of knowledge of good and evil. Admittedly the prohibition comes with a dire warning: 'in the day that you eat of it you shall die.' But the warning is not a threat. It is designed to protect his life, and moreover it gives him moral responsibility and the beginnings of a more mature relationship with his Creator. Now he has the freedom to obey or disobey. Before the prohibition obedience had no meaning. Now it has, and the man can choose life or death. He is not his Maker's puppet.

However, he enjoys no 'blissful ease', for he has a job to do: he must till the garden and watch over it. Later in the story man's work will become drudgery. It is not that yet. Here it is designed to give him a sense of responsibility and of purpose and fulfilment. Through his work the Garden can become his garden also. This story places a high value on work, as some of our other notions of paradise do not.

Secondly, it cannot be said that all manner of things are well. The man is lonely. He does not express his loneliness, but God recognizes it, and means to banish it. So the animals and birds are created! This is still a story concerned with human beings, not with the created order as a whole. The animals and birds appear on the scene because of the demands of the plot. The storyteller is not interested in them for their own sake, but as creatures which might possibly cure the man's loneliness. God brings them to the man, species by species, for him to identify and give them their names. At once we see what a measure of responsibility and freedom God has given the man. In

Genesis 1 God did all the naming. Here the man is doing God's work, and he is the one who will decide which animal or bird is a suitable companion and partner. The way God is described in the story is unusually bold, and here it is at its boldest. We are given the sense that God is experimenting, that he genuinely does not know what will suit the man. The man will choose, and he, God, does not know what his choice will be. Such theology might seem naïve. In truth we are not used to such audacity, and can easily miss its profundity. The freedom of the man pictured here is genuine and complete. His choices will make a difference, they will change things. He does not deal with a God who clings on to control of events, for whom everything is already mapped out, but with a God who, as in Genesis 1, shares power with him. He is called into mutual relationship with this God, and such relationship involves uncertainty and vulnerability *on both sides*. It is daring talk . . . and it will end in Calvary.

We have not come to the end of the writer's audacity. He represents God's experiment as failing! He brings to the man a vast and brilliantly varied procession of creatures, yet none of them suits. The goats and the camels and the lizards simply will not do, nor will the eagles or the red-rumped swallows. God, however, is not at a loss. In Genesis 1 creation was not complete until a creature was made in God's image. Here in Genesis 2 the Garden will not be complete, nor will the man, until a new creature is made in man's image. So woman is made, and the man greets her with a cry of joyful surprise. With her wonderful appearing this story of creation reaches its climax. There is companionship and partnership in the Garden now. The man and the woman are head over heels in love with one another (only if we suppose that does verse 24 make sense), they are husband and wife, and with their love and commitment to one another all manner of things are at last well.

Thoughtless disobedience and its consequences

They are not well for long. The writer leaves us no time to dwell on the couple's happiness. He hints at it further by telling us of their lack of shame, but that leads him straight into a play on words which has dark forebodings. The man and woman are 'naked', *'arummim* in the Hebrew. The serpent is *'arum*, 'clever', 'cunning'. In Genesis 1 human beings were given dominion over the animals. Here they are exposed to an animal's cunning, and are about to fall victim to it.

The serpent is not the Devil. It is not the embodiment of evil. It is simply the most cunning of the creatures God has made. That is all. We must be careful to respect the terms of the story. Jesus told his followers to be 'wise as serpents': the cunning of the serpent was and still is proverbial.

The serpent slips on to the stage of the story without our noticing, and at once we find it in a dialogue with the woman. The serpent talks, not because it is not really a serpent at all but something much more sinister, but simply because the storyteller has turned to fable. In fables, as we know from Aesop, animals are given to talking.

The creature's question seems innocent enough. Certainly the woman catches nothing untoward in it. To her the words 'Did God say, "You shall not eat of any tree of the garden"?' seem like passing the time of the day, and to an apparently straight question she gives a straight answer. 'We may eat of the fruit of the trees of the garden; but God said, "You shall not eat of the fruit of the tree which is in the midst of the garden, neither shall you touch it, lest you die." ' She quotes the prohibition delivered to her husband, and she gets it exactly right, while adding the words, 'neither shall you touch it'. A lot has been written about her addition by those who would make her the villain of the piece and thus blame it all on the weaker (notice that!) sex. 'See how she presumes to add to the divine command!' they say. 'Not content with the words of God, she has to improve on them! What arrogance!' To which we can reply, 'What nonsense!' The story has given us no cause to read that into the woman's words. All we know about her is that she is all that the man desires, that they are in love with one another in complete self-giving, and that she is wide open to the serpent's cunning. Her words do not represent an attempt to improve on God's. Quite the reverse, they reveal that she understands the prohibition.

To the Israelites the holy was dangerous. It was hedged about with rules and regulations designed to protect the unwary. Sinai, when God appears on it in Exodus, is so holy that barriers have to be put around its base to protect the people. God, we are told, instructs Moses what to say to them: 'Take care not to go up the mountain, or even to touch the edge of it. Anyone who touches the mountain shall be put to death' (Exod. 19.12). In the narrative of 2 Samuel, when David is bringing the ark, the most holy object the Israelites knew, into Jerusalem, a man called Uzzah puts out his hand to stop it slipping off the ox-cart. He touches the ark and is killed on the spot (2 Sam. 6.6–7). We may think these passages tell us more about the ancient Israelites' notions of the holy than about God, but they are crucial for our interpretation of the woman's reply. The words she inserts reveal she has grasped that the tree is holy, set apart in the Garden for God's purposes, and is not there for her purposes or her husband's. God has surrounded it with prohibition for their own protection.

The serpent, however, thinks otherwise. Its initial question was not as innocent as it seemed. Though the woman did not catch its sinister undertones, not, at least in her conscious mind, it introduced the idea of a God who might prohibit the couple from eating *any* of the fruit in the Garden, and might thus rob them of their ready supply of food. It suggested a God who might cruelly and indeed dangerously tantalize. Now the serpent's response to the woman's reply speaks more openly of a God who tell lies and is intent on looking after his own narrow interests. 'Of course you will not die!' it tells the woman. 'For God knows that when you eat of it your eyes will be opened, and you will be like God, knowing good and evil.' The prohibition set round the tree is not meant to protect the life of the man and the woman, according to this serpent, but to guard God's monopoly of power. When God told them they would die if they ate the fruit, he was lying. That is the argument, and it is sufficient. The woman takes the forbidden fruit and eats, and gives some to her husband, and he eats also.

But it is not quite as simple as that. The story does not say that the woman agrees with all the serpent has said. She takes the fruit only because she sees that the tree is 'good for food . . . a delight to the eyes and . . . to be desired to make one wise'. What the serpent has done is to rob the tree of its holiness for her. She sees it no longer as something set aside for God's purposes, but as something to serve her own interests. Those interests are modest enough. She wants a little food, a little aesthetic pleasure, a little cleverness and prudence. She does not pick up the words of the serpent about becoming like God. Her ambitions do not rise nearly that far. She grabs for the fruit before she really hears what the snake is saying. She does not stop to think. There is no towering hubris here, no attempt to storm heaven and seize God's place, no attempt to step beyond the limits of the human condition. Like the men who hammer home the nails on Calvary, she does not know what she is doing, and she does not think enough of the consequences. God gave no reason for the prohibition round the tree. The woman in fact worked it out for herself, but now she prefers not to trust her own judgement, but instead that of a serpent she does not wait to understand. Her action is, as others have seen, 'completely natural', 'perfectly human'. That is what is so disarming about it. If the woman were a monster, we could comfort ourselves by saying that we would not have done as she did. The truth of the matter is that even when we are very far from our worst we are uncomfortably like her.

Genesis 1 gave human beings dominion over the animals. Genesis 3 has a woman and a man trapped in the coils of a serpent's cunning. There is a tragic irony to it all. Genesis 1 spoke of human beings made in the image of God. Genesis 3 presents a serpent wooing them with fine words about being 'like God'. After Genesis 1 they are like God already! We see now the sparks these two stories strike off one another.

There is yet more irony in the results of the couple's actions. The serpent promised them that their eyes would be opened, and indeed they are. Yet all they see is their own nakedness! They were naked before, but then it was natural. Now it is something to hide, a sign of their own defencelessness and vulnerability. They were defenceless before, but they did not feel defenceless, for they saw nothing to defend themselves against. Now they feel exposed, because things are not to be trusted any more, and God himself makes them afraid. Their sense of security is gone.

The serpent promised them knowledge which would make them mistress and master of their lives (such mastery is what knowledge of good and evil means). Yet all they can think of doing is to stitch themselves aprons from fig leaves! God will have to clothe them again before they leave Eden. Their pathetic tailoring would be laughable, if only the situation were not so tragic.

All is spoiled. Exposed and bewildered they attempt to hide from God, and then, faced with what they have done, they pass the blame on to another. The man blames the woman, the woman the serpent. The relationship between the man and the woman is spoiled. Joyful surprise and mutual love are replaced by recrimination. The relationship between the couple and the animals, whose harmony Genesis 1 spoke of so clearly, is spoiled also in so far as they and the serpent are at odds with one another.

What God declares in his judgement only confirms what has already taken place, and makes clear its implications. The serpent was once declared 'cunning', 'arum; now it is 'cursed', 'arur. There will be lethal enmity between it and human beings. The woman will long for her husband, but where once she was his equal, now she is to be his subordinate. Mutual self-giving is tainted with subjection and the need to obey. In Genesis 1, in the world of God's making, human beings, both male and female, had dominion over the animals. Now in the garden of the couple's spoiling, it is decreed that man will rule over woman. Nor is that the end of the woman's anguish. Nothing in ancient Israel brought greater honour to a woman than the bearing of children to her husband. This woman will indeed have children, but now in most terrible pain. Her moments of greatest fulfilment and achievement will be clouded with the pain of labour. It will be much the same for the man. He means to find his sense of fulfilment and achievement in his work, but that will now become back-breaking toil. No more the easy harmonious relationship between the fertile world of plants and human beings. No more easy pickings, but instead a constant battle against an unyielding soil until the man's dying day. In Genesis 1 God had only words of blessing for what he had made. Now he lays a curse on the ground and on the serpent too.

The story of Gensis 3 is unutterably sad, and there is sadness yet to come, for the man and woman are driven out from the Garden, and the way back is barred to them. Eden in this story is not the place where God dwells. But it is the place where human beings might bump into him in the cool of the day. Outside Eden meeting God is problematic. Men and women will have to live in hope that God will search them out. No longer is there an inevitability about the encounter.

Many have said that the imposition of death is part of the couple's punishment, but that is not the case. They were not created immortal. That is made quite clear when God denies them access to the tree of life *lest they become* immortal. Certainly death is mentioned in those words 'You are dust and to dust you shall return.' But they do not introduce death as a new phenomenon, only as the end point of the man's life of toil.

There is a bitter irony, even sarcasm in the words of God which introduce his banning the couple from the tree of life and from the Garden. 'Behold,' he says 'the man has become like one of us, knowing good and evil . . .' That is precisely what the couple have *not* become. God means the very opposite of what he says. The words bear the full weight of his bitter disappointment and sense of loss. Yet if we recall Genesis 1 and its pronouncement about human beings being made in God's image and likeness, then a further layer of irony is exposed. God's words express at one and the same time what is demonstrably false and what has been true all along. The compiler of Genesis who put the two stories of creation together greatly heightened the tragedy of the second. His too was work of sheer genius.

It might seem to us that the sentences passed by God in this story are intolerably harsh. Let us remember that things are already spoiled before the sentences are ever pronounced. This is obvious from the first words spoken by the man to God. They are the very first words we have yet heard in these creation stories addressed to God by a human being, and in their great simplicity they encapsulate the tragedy of the human condition: 'I heard the sound of thee in the garden, and I was afraid because I was naked; and I hid myself.' It is obvious also from God's having to remind the man that he has infringed a divine command: 'Have you eaten of the tree of which I commanded you not to eat?' (He will have to remind him again when passing sentence.) It is clearer still from the veiled accusation in the man's reply: 'The woman *whom thou gavest to be with me*, she gave me fruit of the tree and I ate.' It is all God's fault now, it would seem, and this from the man who greeted woman at her making with such joy!

What is unexpected about God's sentences is not their harshness but their leniency. '. . . in the day that you eat of it you shall die.' Those were the terms of the prohibition. Unlike Uzzah, the man and woman do not die. The holy does not, after all, have its almost magical power to destroy those who touch it. And God's apparent change of mind reveals that indeed the prohibition was meant to protect the man and the woman. Despite its infringement he shields them from the harm of the holy, and protects them also against the rigours of life outside Eden by making them coats of skins. Once beyond Eden the first thing the woman will do is conceive and bear a son 'with the help of the Lord' (4.1). They will not leave God's protection behind in Eden, nor will the words of blessing spoken in Genesis 1 have lost their power. This God will not let the man and the woman go. Other stories in the Old Testament bear even more eloquent witness to his tenacity.

The familiarity of the Garden

Genesis 2–3 is on one level about an individual man and woman. On another it is, as we have said already, about Man and Woman. It is about the human condition, not as it once was, but as it is, and as we long for it to be. It is written as if it was about the remote past, but it is more about the present and the future.

The world of the Garden is familiar enough. The sentences passed by God at the end reflect the world we know (except that we are rather better informed now about what snakes eat!). The joys of childbearing and motherhood are indeed mixed with pain, and work too often is drudgery. The battle simply to survive is for many a fierce one, and life is lived at odds with things. Even the most comfortable have the sense that things are not as they should be. Women have generally still not achieved equality with men, and subservience and the need to obey are still a feature of many marriages. (It is astonishing that a story coming out of such a male-dominated society as ancient Israel should protest that only full equality belongs to the world of God's making.) Furthermore we are familiar with the sense that encounter with God is problematic. It is not only Jews from the holocaust who have had the keen sense of God's absence from the world, and who have caught a glimpse of his retreating back. Rootlessness is a common affliction, or else a sense of not being rooted where we belong, of not yet being at home with God, able to bump into him as he walks in the cool of the day.

Yet still men and women fall head over heels in love with one another. Relationships of remarkable depth and closeness can still be enjoyed between human beings and animals. The fertility of the earth is in many place still remarkable. The sense that beneath it all, all is well, still comes over many people, even in harsh and cruel circumstances. And the intimacy with God so beautifully expressed in the accounts of the making of the man and woman can still at times be enjoyed.

The story might give us the impression that the real world is that of chapter 3 and the Garden of chapter 2 is only a dream. By the grace and mercy of God the experience of very many human beings would suggest that that impression is wrong and that, in fact, despite the story's ending, we still have one foot in Eden. One Day, at God's Ending, we will complete our return, for God himself will take us back there.

2

GOD'S PROMISES ON THE BRINK and a hero brought down to earth with a bump

(Genesis 22—23)

The story so far, Act I: From creation to Abraham

With Genesis 1–3 we could begin with Genesis 1. With the two stories of Abraham in Genesis 22–23 we cannot properly start with them, but must quickly trace 'the story so far'. Only if we put them into their context in the larger narrative, can we see what is going on and feel their full force.

But where does the story-so-far begin? Not with Abraham, but back where we have already been, in the World of God's making and the Garden of his planting. It starts with a vision of a world where all is in God's good order, where all is very beautiful and God's delight. It begins with a Garden where, with the creation of the woman, all is harmony and joy, intimacy and self-giving. So very quickly, as we have seen, this is spoiled. And so very quickly beyond Eden things get much worse.

No sooner are we out of Eden than we find ourselves in a field stained with a brother's blood (4.1–16). Abel's offering is accepted by God and Cain's rejected. As with the prohibition to do with the tree in the midst of the Garden, God gives no explanation. He chooses to remain inscrutable. But Cain immediately interprets his act as an acceptance of his brother and a rejection of him. The man in Eden, Cain's father, at first accepted God's prohibition without question, and he and the woman only misread God's motives when prompted by the snake. Cain leaps at once to disastrous conclusions, and the consequence is not the eating of fruit now, but jealousy and cold, calculated murder, fratricide. When he is challenged he lays the blame, like his father, at God's door, but with a new and terrible cynicism and with an outright lie. To God's question, 'Where is Abel your brother?' he replies, 'I do not know,' and then, 'Am *I* my brother's keeper?' (There is an emphasis in the Hebrew not generally conveyed in our versions.) 'You, God, are my brother's keeper, and look what a mess you have made of the job!' That is Cain's unspoken accusation. Even without it his question encapsulates all that is selfish and ruthless among human beings. With it, it reaches towards the dead centre of the tragic side of human nature.

After this it comes as little surprise to learn that 'the earth was corrupt in God's sight, and the earth was filled with violence' (Gen. 6.11). In the most terrifying story in all Scripture God decides to begin again with a single family, this time with one whose head, Noah, has shown some signs of righteousness. The Flood of Genesis is no ordinary flood on an extraordinary scale. To suggest that it could be or has been 'proved' by archaeologists is to do the story a great disservice. It describes something of quite another order. God withdraws the limits he imposed in Genesis 1 on the vast waters, both those placed above the firmament and those below. Once more they become waters of chaos and engulf and destroy God's whole creation. Only the continued succession of days and nights, and a crowded ark bobbing on the surface of the waters, prevent a complete return to the state of things before God began his great work of creation.

After the Flood is over, God blesses Noah and his sons with the familiar words, 'Be fruitful and multiply, and fill the earth' (9.1). We are not quite back where we began, for human dominion over the earth is different now. Then it was a case of keeping things in God's fine order, and only plants and their fruit were to supply human beings with food. Now men are to be hunters and predators. 'Every moving thing that lives shall be food for you,' God tells Noah and his sons. The declared results remind us more readily of the spoiled world of Genesis 3 than those of Genesis 1 or 2: 'The fear of you and the dread of you shall be upon every beast of the earth, and upon every bird of the air, upon everything that creeps on the ground, and all fish of the sea' (9.2).

In other respects, however, the new beginning, the new creation, for that is what it is, seems bright enough. But there is a second and hidden flaw. The human beings who survive the Flood come from the old corrupt, violent order. Noah himself is beyond reproach, it is true. His sons, however, are not, and almost immediately Noah is humiliated and disgraced by one of them, and the story returns to the language of the curse (9.20–27). Noah's cursing Canaan reminds us all too clearly of the cursing of Cain.

As it did after Cain, the scope of the story now enlarges rapidly. From the sons of Noah emerge a host of peoples, and some, migrating from the east, settle on a plain in the land of Shinar (11. 1–9). 'Come,' they say to one another, 'Let us build ourselves a city, and a tower with its top in the heavens, and let us make a name for ourselves, lest we be scattered abroad upon the face of the whole earth' (11.4). Who are they afraid of? Of other peoples? If so, then we are reminded of the violent earth before the Flood. Of God? Then we must recall the fear of the couple in the Garden. Whichever the case, things are so awry that God himself is afraid and immediately jumps to the conclusion that they mean to seize the power that properly belongs to him. There are stories in other places of men storming heaven. The story of the Tower of Babel is not one of them. The human aspirations expressed are modest by comparison, like those of the woman underneath the tree in the midst of the Garden. But God 'misreads' what is going on (how is that for audacious storytelling!) and is conscious only of the threat to his domain. '. . . this is only the beginning of what they will do; and nothing that they propose to do will now be impossible for them' (11.6). So he confuses their language and scatters them over the face of all the earth. The fears of the city builders were, it seems, justified after all, and it was God they had to fear. It is as if God, embittered by the recalcitrance of humanity, has turned to behaving in the same manner as that imputed to him by the serpent in the Garden in its dialogue with the woman. It is as if he is intent only on protecting his own interests. But that cannot be so (not, at least, if we take note of the rest of Scripture), and indeed it is not. The story begins again.

The story so far, Act II: From Abraham to Isaac

For a third time it starts with a single family, indeed, as in the Garden, with a single couple, Abraham and Sarah. There are no children to spoil things as there were with Noah. There seems no prospect of children, since Sarah is barren. What Abraham receives instead is a command, 'Go from your country and your kindred and your father's house to the land that I will show you', and promises: 'And I will make of you a great nation, and I will bless you, and make your name great, so that you will be a blessing. I will bless those who bless you, and him who curses you I will curse; and by you all the families of the earth shall bless themselves' (12.1–3). There is no explicit mention of a child to be born to him and Sarah, and there will be none for another three chapters (not until 15.4). But none of the promises can be fulfilled without first a child being born, or, to be more precise in Abraham's patriarchal world, a son.

The Abraham narratives are dominated by the birth of this son, or rather by its delay. Not until they are almost over is he born. Meanwhile his birth comes to seem more and more impossible and Abraham on several occasions brings everything to the brink of disaster.

Abraham has gone down in Christian tradition as one of the great men of faith. St Paul and the writer of the Letter to the Hebrews are primarily responsible for that, but their judgement is derived not so much from Genesis as from Jewish writings of the period between the Old and New Testaments which turned Abraham into a plaster saint. The portrayal of Abraham in Genesis is much more complex. It avoids stereotype, it is closer to reality, and though less comforting perhaps, it is much more interesting, and in the end more profound.

Abraham certainly begins magnificently. When told to leave all behind, his past, his roots, his culture, his sense of belonging, his status and position in society and the family, the friendship, support and love of those close to him, everything except for Sarah, his wife, and Lot, his nephew, he goes without a moment's hesitation. But soon he is forced by famine to go down to Egypt, and when he is about to cross the border he resorts to a ploy which knocks him straight off any pedestal we might have erected for him. He says to Sarah, 'I know that you are a woman beautiful to behold, and when the Egyptians see you, they will say, "This is his wife"; then they will kill me, but they will let you live. Say you are my sister, that it may go well with me because of you, and that my life may be spared on your account' (12.11b–13). We do not need to be feminists to see this as blatant and shocking selfishness. He is intent only on saving his own skin. Sarah's feelings and the consequences for her are not considered. But it is considerably worse than that, as the story quickly makes clear. Sarah is taken into the Pharaoh's harem. What now the prospects for the promises of God? It is true we have not yet been told, nor has Abraham, that Sarah will be the mother of the son on whom everything depends. But we have heard of no other wife. It appears that the promises of God, his plans for a new beginning for his world, are locked up in a Pharaoh's palace. God has to go to the rescue. The immediate result is a confrontation between an angry and bewildered Pharaoh and Abraham. Abraham, a rootless nomad, meets the king of the most sophisticated culture in the Ancient Near East, one regarded by his people as a god incarnate. It would seem to be all over. But Abraham still has God on his side, and the Pharaoh lets him go, and Sarah with him.

It is a narrow escape, but a few chapters later we find Abraham doing it all over again, this time in the city of Gerar (ch. 20). The king there is Abimelech, and Sarah finds herself in another royal harem. A seond time God has to intervene. In the course of Abimelech's questioning of Abraham it emerges that he has been claiming Sarah is his sister at every place they have been! Undoubtedly there is humour here, but however much we laugh we must not forget what is at stake, nor fail to appreciate the danger into which Abraham has brought not only Sarah, but the grand purposes of God.

In another story, between those concerning Abraham's escapades in Egypt and Gerar, we find him going to war (ch. 14). Lot is captured in a sacking of Sodom, and to rescue him Abraham goes into battle with 318 men against the combined armies of four kings who have already routed those of five others. Family loyalty demands he attempt to rescue his nephew, even if it means, as the story suggests it does, a round trip of between three and four hundred miles. The nomadic tribesmen of the contemporary Middle East would still understand this story well enough. But given its setting, we must not allow ourselves to be blinded by Abraham's bravery, nor, when we read of the resounding success of his venture, by his military prowess. The son on whom all depends is still not conceived. Abraham does not just risk his life in this campaign. He wears the promises of God underneath his battle dress, and puts them in danger of being hacked to pieces with his own body.

As the Abraham narrative wends its way through these and other events, the birth of the son of the promise is made to appear more and more unlikely. We had notice of Sarah's barrenness even before it properly got under way (11.30). At the start of chapter 16 we are reminded of it again, and things seem so hopeless now that Sarah urges Abraham to have a child by her Egyptian maid, Hagar. According to ancient custom it would be possible for Sarah as wife to claim the child as her own. A child is duly conceived, but before ever it is born, there is a breakdown of relationships between Sarah and

Hagar, and Hagar has to flee into the desert. She flees for her life, yet she goes to almost certain death. It is vital to remember that we have not yet been told that Sarah will be the mother of the son of the promise. For all we know, and for all Abraham and Sarah know too, it is Hagar who carries in her womb the plans of God for the redemption of the world. Yet it is she whom Abraham hands over to Sarah to do with as she pleases, and who is treated so cruelly by her mistress that she is forced to escape into the sands. There is no thought anywhere for Hagar, for her unborn child, or for the purposes of God. God is left to look after all of them by himself. As a result Hagar is saved and restored to Abraham, and her child, Ishmael, is safely born. Soon we learn he is not the son of the promise, nor is Hagar to be the mother of that child. The larger purposes of God were not at risk of dying of thirst in the desert after all. Yet the story of Hagar's flight furnishes another example of Abraham treating the promises of God very lightly, to put it at its mildest.

When we, the hearers and readers of the narrative, and Abraham, are told by God that he will have a son by Sarah, we learn that Abraham will be a hundred years old when the child is born and Sarah is already ninety (17.17). They inhabit a world emerging from a period when human beings are said to have lived for hundreds of years. Abraham's grandfather, Nahor, is said to have lived 148 years, and Abraham was born when his father, Terah, was seventy (11.24–6). But when Abraham hears that he and Sarah will have a child he finds the news preposterous. He laughs, and clings to the notion that Ishmael is the child of the promise (a child whom he had allowed when still unborn to be driven into the wilderness to die!). God has to repeat his promise: 'No, but Sarah your wife shall bear you a son, and you shall call his name Isaac' (17.19).

In the next chapter it is Sarah's turn to hear the happy news (Abraham does not seem to have passed it on!). God appears to her and Abraham in the form of three men. (What is there is God himself. What they *see* is three men – the Hebrew makes this clearer than the English.) Sarah overhears her husband being told that she will have a son in the spring. She is past the menopause and she and Abraham have long since given up sexual intercourse. Like her husband she laughs the news out of court (18.10–15).

With Abraham's and Sarah's laughter the storyteller is indulging in another play on words. Isaac, the name to be given the promised son, means 'he laughs'. Thus their laughter is prophetic. It is also readily understandable. Their laughter is our laughter. The promise *is* ridiculous. Yet their laughter remains open to censure. Sarah is caught out laughing and promptly denies it. At least she does not recognize who she is talking to, for God is in strange disguise. Abraham, in the previous chapter, is in no doubt at all. He laughs while prostrate before his God, in the attitude of reverence and worship. Mocking laughing in this position is truly shocking. God is treated with loud contempt.

Abraham and Sarah in these chapters are ambiguous characters. They are by no means all bad, but they are certainly not all good. Despite their astounding obedience at the start of their story, they belong to the old order, and betray its features: deceit, fear, including fear of God, selfishness, thoughtlessness, recklessness, cruelty and shocking disbelief. This is all too familiar. If God is truly to begin again, then he must start with a child born out of the blue, a child most decidedly of his making. With Isaac there is a possibility of a new order being established. With Isaac God can look forward to a world over which he can again clap his hands in delight. When finally he is born, Sarah cries, 'God has made laughter for me' (21.6). Looking at the sweep of the whole narrative from Genesis 1 outwards, we can say that God has made laughter for himself also, and for the whole world. Isaac is God's laughter incarnate.

That is why the story of the binding of Isaac in chapter 22 is so bewildering. On several occasions before Isaac's birth we have seen the purposes of God brought to the edge of disaster by Abraham. Now we read of the most direct and serious threat of all. And it comes from God himself!

We have arrived at chapter 22, but before we deal with it in detail, we must look quickly at another story that lies between Isaac's birth and his coming so soon and so close to death.

Sarah's laughter turns to ruthless jealousy (21.8ff.). When Isaac is still very small, she sees Ishmael playing with him. The scene is an entirely innocent one, yet it provokes Sarah to her greatest act of cruelty. 'Cast out this slave woman with her son,' she commands Abraham, 'for the son of this slave woman shall not be heir with my son Isaac.' The order is uncompromising, and disconcerts Abraham. But God then intervenes, not on the side of Hagar and Ishmael, as we might expect, but in support of Sarah. Hagar and her son are indeed to be cast out, and God explains the place their banishment will take in his larger purposes. Ishmael will be the ancestor of a nation, but one quite distinct from Isaac's people.

So Hagar finds herself once more in the desert. Her meagre supply of water runs out, and she puts Ishmael in the shade of a bush to die. She sits some way off, and waits for death. Here the story turns, for the child cries and is heard by God. The 'angel of God' calls from heaven: 'What troubles you, Hagar? Fear not; for God has heard the voice of the lad where he is. Arise, lift up the lad . . . for I will make him a great nation.' The assurances made to Abraham were not empty ones, as they cannot be where God is concerned. God shows Hagar a well. Thirst is banished, and the desert becomes their home. When Ishmael is old enough to marry, Hagar not surprisingly finds a wife for him in her own country of Egypt. She will have no more truck with Abraham and his kind!

It is a poignant story this, and an unnerving one. We will find it echoed in several places in chapter 22.

The binding of Isaac

Near the beginning of Shakespeare's *King Lear* we, the audience, learn that Lear's two elder daughters, Goneril and Regan, are false, while his youngest, Cordelia, is true. Goneril and Regan bear their father only flattering words, and lust for their own power. Cordelia loves him. We know the truth of the matter. But Lear does not, and we sit and watch helplessly as his not knowing leads to chaos in his kingdom, to madness, and to death. Shakespeare's technique, to let us into a secret that the hero will only discover for himself at the end, is a common one in playwriting and storytelling. It is the technique employed in Genesis 22, and it creates enormous tension and suspense in the narrative, even though the ending is mercifully not that of high tragedy.

'After these things God tested Abraham.' That is how it starts. We at once are privy to the secrets of God's mind. But Abraham is not. He will learn of them at the end, when it is all over, and even then only indirectly. Meanwhile we, and God too, must wait to see if he passes the test or not. After the stories of the last few chapters, since the point when the promises were first given, our confidence in Abraham's reliability has been shaken nearly to pieces.

God calls to Abraham, 'Abraham!' and he replies, 'Here am I.' In chapter 12, when it all began, there was only monologue. By now God and Abraham have been through a great deal together. Dialogue is appropriate. Next, as before, a command. 'Take your son, your only son, whom you love, Isaac, and go to the land of

Moriah, and offer him there as a burnt offering upon one of the mountains of which I shall tell you.' The storyteller himself would have us recall the command of chapter 12. The Hebrew words translated 'go' in 22.2 are *lech l'cha*. Nowhere else does this phrase occur in the Old Testament except in 12.1. *Lech* means 'go' by itself. *L'cha*, literally 'for yourself', softens the command. There is a courtesy in the divine speech, an appeal for Abraham's co-operation, that was distinctly lacking in chapter 21 and Sarah's abrupt 'Cast out this slave woman with her son.' But courtesy is not everything. The divine command is truly terrible. It was bad enough when Abraham was asked to sacrifice his past. Now he is being asked to sacrifice his future, and, if we remember the course of the story so far, God's future for the world. The horror and the pain of it are hinted at in the progression, 'your son, your only son, whom you love, Isaac' (this is the order in the Hebrew). Isaac is not Abraham's only son. But God is not lying. He is simply looking at things from Abraham's point of view. Ishmael was driven away with his mother into the desert, and has not returned. For all Abraham knows, he is dead. God's calling Isaac his 'only son' would seem to confirm it. The words add horror to horror.

In chapter 12 Abraham was given a reason for his going, for the promises came hard on the heels of the command. Here, like the man in the Garden when the prohibition was delivered, or Cain when his offering was rejected, he receives no explanation at all. Of course, *we* know that Abraham is being tested. But 'Take . . . go . . . offer' is all Abraham gets. We now expect protest, more dialogue. There is none. Instead we have the details of Abraham's preparations. He gets up early in the morning, saddles his ass, cuts the wood for the sacrifice, and taking two young servants and Isaac with him, he sets off for the place of which God has told him. As his going was in chapter 12, it is all so matter-of-fact! No space was devoted then to Abraham's feelings, nor is it here. No space is devoted here to anybody's feelings, not to Isaac's, nor the servants'. As for Sarah, she is entirely forgotten in this story. In chapter 17 it seems that Abraham did not tell Sarah that she would be having a child. Now he does not tell her that he is going to put a knife to that child's throat and burn his body to ashes. If he does tell her, then we do not hear about it, nor do we know of Sarah's reaction. The story's silence concerning Sarah is one of its most terrible aspects. As its days go by, we are left to imagine for ourselves Sarah's anxiety. One thing is certain: if Abraham has not told her of the divine command, then even her worst fears will not allow her to guess what is afoot.

There is one curious feature of Abraham's preparations. It is a three-day journey to the land of Moriah, yet he cuts the wood for Isaac's funeral pyre before he sets off, and takes it all the way with him. Isaac will himself carry it up the mountain where the sacrifice is to be made. Is there really no wood to be found on the way, or even on the mountain itself? We cannot answer that question. All we can say is that the burden of the wood adds further poignancy to an already heart-rending story, and throughout the journey acts as an all too visible reminder to Abraham of the act he is about to commit.

The journey is a long one, but it is hurried over in a few words. Once Abraham can see the place where he will kill his son, the pace of the narrative slows right down. He tells the servants to stay put, and says that he and 'the lad' will 'go yonder and worship', and then return. What unspoken horror is in that word 'worship'! No wonder that Abraham cannot bring himself to name Isaac, or even refer to him as his son. He dissembles when he talks of their return, too. He expects to come back alone. But the servants cannot be told that. Nor can Isaac.

More reporting of preparations. The wood is taken off the ass, and laid on Isaac. He is a beast of burden, an animal for sacrifice, and like a man on the way to Calvary bears on his back the means for his death.

'So they went both of them together.' Twice these words occur in this last part of the journey, and frame a little dialogue of extreme simplicity, which surely must rank as one of the great moments in biblical storytelling. Isaac addresses 'his father' Abraham: 'My father!' 'Here am I, my son.' 'Behold, the fire and the wood; but where is the lamb for a burnt offering?' 'God will provide himself the lamb for a burnt offering, my son.' Twice the word 'father'; twice the phrase 'my son'. Thus the dialogue and its frame emphasize the bond between the two of them, and thereby further underline the horror of the sacrifice of which they speak.

There is great irony in those last words of Abraham's, 'God will provide . . .' Some have seen them as a fine declaration of faith, but they are not. 'The lamb' which Abraham means is Isaac. God has commanded him to sacrifice his son. That is all he knows. When they reach their goal, Abraham goes calmly about the business of preparing Isaac for slaughter. He does not hunt high and low for an animal to use instead. He gives us no sign that he believes God will provide a substitute at the last moment, no sign of a conviction that all will be well in the end. Does this mean that this story is not about faith, but faithlessness? Does it mean that Abraham no longer has any trust in God's promises? The story does not allow us to answer those questions for certain. But if Abraham's trust has gone, God has given him cause. In chapter 21, in the account of Sarah's cruelty and Hagar's and Ishmael's banishment, God appeared to Abraham on the side of the oppressor, not the oppressed. Though he reassured him about the boy's future, his calling Isaac his 'only son' when he commands him to go to the land of Moriah might well suggest those assurances were empty and meant nothing. Abraham would seem to be dealing with a God who has his own cruelty, and who cannot be relied upon to keep his promises. After all the command to sacrifice Isaac would appear of itself to back that up. The promises of chapter 12, repeated at intervals before Isaac's birth, must mean nothing.

But Isaac has no knowledge of the divine command his father has received. He must take the words 'God will provide himself the lamb for a burnt offering' at their face value. For him they *are* a declaration of faith, and an answer to his bewilderment. In the end his taking the words literally will be proved correct. Though Abraham does not know it, he has spoken the truth! It is Isaac, who understands nothing of what is going on, who in fact understands here, while his father, who thought he understood, understands nothing. That is the greatest irony of all.

When they reach the place of sacrifice, the details of the final preparations are given in the same matter-of-fact way that the initial ones were. The spot is not already a sanctuary. Abraham must first build an altar. (How the agony is prolonged!) The wood is laid on the altar, Isaac is bound and then 'put' (the word in the Hebrew is as colourless as that: it is as if he is an object for slaughter, no longer a human being, let alone Abraham's son) on the wood. All is now ready. Abraham puts forth his hand, and takes the knife 'to slay his son'. The words balance the earlier 'put', and remind us of the truth. They begin to give the colour back to Isaac's cheeks, but they are as far as the storyteller will go. As at the start of this story there is no mention of the feelings of those involved. Isaac, unlike Ishmael underneath the bush in the desert, does not cry out. There is no protest from him or his father. No words of any kind pass between them. The appalling actions are done in complete silence. It is so strange, it is like the awesome silence which in the minds of the ancient Israelites sometimes preceded divine revelation.

And so indeed it is. The 'angel of the Lord' calls from heaven, just as he did when Ishmael was so near death. 'Abraham, Abraham!' The name is called twice now, for the matter is doubly urgent. 'Here am I.' The silence is broken, and dialogue resumed. Then another command: 'Do not lay your hand on the lad or do anything to him; for now I know that you fear God, seeing you have not withheld your son, your only son, from me.' Abraham has passed the test, Isaac is saved, and the purposes of God are brought back from the edge of the abyss. Earlier in the story Abraham lifted up his eyes and saw ahead of him the place where he thought he would kill his son. Now he lifts up his eyes again, and sees the animal that is his son's salvation, a ram caught in a thicket. He sacrifices the ram, and then gives a name to the place, 'The Lord provides!' The word is the same as he used before in his dialogue with Isaac. Then he did not mean what he said. Now he does. The name is a cry of relief and joy. It marks the only point in the entire story where Abraham's feelings are allowed to come anywhere near the surface.

The angel of God (at this stage in Israelite writing just another way of referring to God himself) calls a second time: 'By myself I have sworn . . . because you have done this, and have not withheld your son, your only son, I will indeed bless you, and I will multiply your descendants as the stars of heaven and as the sand which is on the seashore. And your descendants shall possess the gate of their enemies, and by your descendants shall all the families find blessing, because you have obeyed my voice.' The old promises are thus repeated, and the threefold use of the word 'descendants' would seem to rub it into the mind of the bewildered Abraham that indeed Isaac is saved.

Making sense of God

But if Abraham is bewildered, so are we. What in heaven's name has been going on? The question is not exactly easy to answer, and is made initially more difficult by the repetition of the promises at the end. On all the occasions they have been made before, they have been unconditional. When first God commanded Abraham to leave everything behind, he did not wait to see the order obeyed before giving the promises. But now, after he has commanded Abraham to leave everything behind a second time, he waits until Abraham has passed the test.

It would seem that the birth of Isaac has made all the difference, and might hold the clue to our question about what has been going on.

While Isaac is still unborn, the promises speak only of the future.

Admittedly we find Abraham as early as chapter 13 walking through the length and breadth of the Promised Land, thus appearing to take legal possession of it. But that act has more to do with the future than the present, as chapter 23 will make abundantly clear. Only with the birth of Isaac does the world of God's promises begin to become reality. In that world there is laughter, joy and fulfilment, but also new demands. The man and woman in the Garden were not free from God's demands. For life with God to be enjoyed there, those demands had to be met. Everything depended on the man's and the woman's obedience. So it was with Noah in God's second beginning, and so it is now with Abraham in his third. Without obedience, all will be spoiled. Without it, when he was first called, God's new plans for the redemption of his world would not have got under way at all. Now that those plans have at last come to some fruition, Abraham's obedience must be tested again. Love always makes demands. We all know that. Complete love, such as God's is, demands all. We know that too, perhaps, though if we do, we do our best to forget it.

Yet in the face of this particular story such sentiments can seem like pious claptrap. The demands made of Abraham here are so very terrible. If we suspected a cruel God in chapter 21, then surely we have got one now.

Any sensitive reading of a story demands a feeling for how far one is permitted to push the significance of its details, and an awareness of those questions that can properly be asked of it, and those which cannot. I suspect that the theology of Genesis 22 is not to be pushed very far, that cautious theology has here been sacrificed on the fine altar of dramatic tension and powerful storytelling. It is one of the glories of the Old Testament that its writers are seldom over-careful about what they say about their God. They prove time and time again the risks they are prepared to take.

There is, however, one thing more to be said. The Abraham narrative has made it abundantly clear that Isaac comes out of God's bright blue. He is sheer gift. The story of his binding makes clear that he remains so, and that he must be accepted as such. Later in the Old Testament we are told how Job, robbed of everything, at first reacts by declaring, 'The Lord gave, and the Lord has taken away; blessed be the name of the Lord' (Job 1.21). Those words may seem too hard for us to take, but God requires Abraham to act them out in the land of Moriah. If he regards Isaac as his own and not God's, as the woman and the man in the Garden came to regard that tree as their own and not God's, then all will be ruined. If he treats his son truly as God's, more God's son than his own, and is prepared to hand him back, then God's new era will surely dawn, and Abraham can give it a fitting name: 'The Lord provides!'

Genesis 22 would teach us not to underestimate the demands of God. It would teach us also not to underestimate the sheer abundance of the world of God's promise. The words of the Johannine Jesus, 'I came that they may have life, and have it abundantly', are in the end apt comment on this story.

Bartering for a burial plot

Genesis 22 has, not surprisingly, provided inspiration to many artists. Among them is the First World War poet, Wilfred Owen, who wrote the following lines, under the title, 'The Parable of the Old Man and the Young'.

> So Abram rose, and clave the wood, and went,
> And took the fire with him, and a knife.
> And as they sojourned both of them together,
> Isaac the first-born spake and said, My Father,
> Behold the preparations, fire and iron,
> But where the lamb for this burnt offering?
> Then Abram bound the youth with belts and straps,
> And builded parapets and trenches there,
> And stretched forth the knife to slay his son.
> When lo! an angel called him out of heaven,
> Saying, Lay not thy hand upon the lad,
> Neither do anything to him. Behold,
> A ram, caught in a thicket by its horns;
> Offer the Ram of Pride instead of him.
> But the old man would not so, but slew his son,
> And half the seed of Europe, one by one.

Owen uses the story of the binding of Isaac to comment on the war in which he was fighting, and has given it a vicious twist at the end. In a very different, but no less brilliant way the compiler of Genesis gives the Abraham narrative a final twist by following the story of the binding by one concerning Abraham's purchase of a burial plot. Abraham's death is not recorded till chapter 25, and he features, too, at the start of chapter 24. But chapter 23 gives us the last piece of true storytelling in which Abraham is centre stage throughout. It occupies a very prominent place in the narrative, therefore, and we might expect something particularly fine and solemn after the heroics of chapter 22. For Abraham was a hero there. Though we found ourselves asking whether the story was about faith or faithlessness, we were left in no doubt about Abraham's stature at the end. He passed God's test, and a test of the severest kind at that, and received God's high praise. Surely the story that follows must sustain the high note that has been reached. But if we think that, we have not reckoned with the mischief of the compiler. He brings Abraham down to earth with a bump, by giving us a subtle piece of comedy in which he features as something of a country bumpkin and gets, to use unsubtle language for a moment, 'right done'!

Sarah is dead, and Abraham must find somewhere to bury her. By the terms of his dealings with God the whole land is his. He has walked the length and breadth of it, taken possession of it. But what goes on between God and the individual is not always taken notice of by society at large. God's 'legal transactions' are not the law of the land, not of Abraham's land at any rate. By the law of the land he is a resident alien (23.4). By the law of the land, not only does he possess none of it, he does not even have the right to own any of it. For that right he must negotiate with the citizens of Hebron. If it is given, it will change his status among them. He will belong. He will no longer be an alien in his own land.

The story concerns itself with those negotiations. To understand it, it helps to have had some experience of a bartering society.

The outcome of bartering is almost bound to be determined by the starting points of the parties involved. In this particular case Abraham is at a very distinct disadvantage. He has a certain reputation in Hebron (though not as much as the exaggerated courtesy of verse 6 would suggest), but no political power. If his legal status is to be changed, he must rely on the generosity of the citizens. To start negotiations having to rely on the generosity of the other party is not to start in the strongest of positions! Furthermore, his need is very great. The ancient Israelites set great store by proper burial. It is imperative for Abraham that a burial site be purchased, and quickly. Sarah's corpse in that climate will not wait. The citizens of Hebron, by contrast, hold all the trump cards. There are many more of them, for a start. They have the political power, they establish and run the legal system. They do not just know the ropes: they *make* the ropes. They also have all the sophistication of city-dwellers. Courtesy and hospitality, it is true, would demand that they pay heed to this alien in his great need but their obligations extend no further than that.

Abraham makes his request: 'Give me land enough among you so that I may bury my dead properly.' He does not mean 'give' in the accepted sense of the word, of course. Such a demand would be unthinkable in the circumstances. He means 'sell', but etiquette leads him to avoid the word. The citizens of Hebron understand what he means, though one of them will use that word 'give' to his own advantage later. 'Bury your dead in the best grave we have,' is their first response. The first response of any seller in a strong position is bound to be an impossible one, and so this is. Abraham, the alien, cannot possibly bury Sarah in their finest grave. The offer would seem at first sight to be an extremely generous one, but those who make it know it cannot be accepted. All it achieves is to give them an air of generosity, and so put Abraham at an even greater disadvantage in the rounds to come. Anyway, it does not fulfil Abraham's requirements. He is asking to buy property among them. He is asking to be no longer an alien. However fine the grave is for Sarah, if it is not his, then his status will not change at all. Furthermore he has a particular site in mind, as he reveals in the next round of the negotiations. '. . . entreat for me Ephron the son of Zohar, that he may give me the cave of Machpelah, which he owns; it is at the end of his field. For the full price let him give it to me in your presence as a possession for a burying place.' Now it is clear what he wants.

Ephron is among the citizens present. The remaining negotiations must be between him and Abraham. It is an uneven match. Ephron picks up Abraham's 'give' and uses it three times in his opening offer. 'No, my lord,' (such courtesy again, and such artful courtesy too, as we shall see!) 'hear me; I give you the field, and I give you the cave that is in it; in the presence of the sons of my people I give it to you; bury your dead.' When Abraham said 'give', he meant 'sell'. When Ephron says 'give', he means 'give' . . . and he does not mean 'give'.

A student at the theological college where I teach once told a most illuminating story when I was conducting a seminar on this passage. He had spent several years in the Sudan and he gave us a tip: 'Never take a taxi there,' he said, 'without fixing the price for the journey before you get in.' On one occasion he had failed to do so, and had had to start negotiating when he got to his destination. 'How much is that?' he had asked. 'Give me whatever you like,' the driver had suggested. 'How about — ?' and he had quoted a ridiculously small sum. My friend, the student, could not have begun to agree to that, and of course the taxi driver would not have allowed him to. At the end of some noisy haggling he had ended up paying the driver way over the odds.

The Ephron of our story, like the Sudanese taxi driver, does not mean what he says, as he makes abundantly clear when Abraham insists on paying a proper price for the field and the cave. 'My lord,' he replies, still with the utmost courtesy, 'listen to me; a piece of land worth four hundred shekels of silver, what is that between you and me? Bury your dead.' There we have it! Slipped in as if it is a mere trifle, a quite exorbitant price! We know just how exorbitant it is from references elsewhere in the Old Testament. Omri, a king of Irsael in the ninth century, for six thousand shekels acquired the entire site for his new capital city of Samaria (1 Kings 16.24). The prophet Jeremiah bought a field at Anathoth and paid just seventeen shekels for it (Jer. 32.9). Of course, an absurd price is exactly what we would have expected Ephron to suggest in the circumstances. Now, surely, the hard bargaining will begin.

But no. Abraham is caught in Ephron's net. He has offered to pay the full market price. Ephron has told him the land is worth four hundred shekels. To refuse to pay that would be tantamount to accusing him of lying, and such an accusation cannot be countenanced in these circumstances. Secondly, to refuse to pay would be to deny the exalted status that Ephron and his fellow Hittites have accorded him. They have called him 'a mighty prince' and 'lord'. Mighty princes can afford to pay four hundred shekels for a cave and a field. Abraham is in search of status in Hebron, and in any case the fear of humiliation will encourage him to pay. Thirdly, and perhaps most importantly, to try to beat Ephron down to a lower price would surely be to heap dishonour on Sarah. He cannot, 'mighty prince' that he is, appear to suggest that she, his 'princess', is not worth four hundred shekels. The silver has to be weighed out, all four hundred shekels of it, and indeed it is.

We could have guessed that Abraham would end up paying over the odds, but not as much as this. The clever Ephron has taken him for a very long ride indeed.

The story of the purchase of Sarah's burial plot is comedy, and comedy frequently takes delight in debunking heroes. Abraham is made to look foolish. But why? Just for entertainment's sake? Well, make no mistake about it, these stories were designed to entertain, and this one clearly meant to amuse. But it is entertainment with a serious intent. The Old Testament does not go in for saints. Genesis does not go in for saints (though Joseph will, perhaps, approach that status). It is too clear-eyed about human nature for that. It is too clear-eyed also about the holiness and the goodness of God. There is only one hero, and he is God. The compiler of Genesis would not have us forget that.

There is one last irony. The purchase of Ephron's field and cave represents the first step towards Israel's actual possession of the Promised Land. It is not exactly an auspicious start!

3

A WRESTLING MATCH WITH GOD and two brothers so nearly reconciled

(Genesis 32—33)

Isaac: the tragedy and the hope

Genesis has very little to tell us about Isaac. We have waited so long for him to be born, and such fine promises rest on his shoulders. Yet apart from the story of his binding, a long account of the finding of a wife for him, for the bulk of which he is off stage, and a story about him on his death-bed which is primarily about his sons, Jacob and Esau, there is but one chapter devoted to him (ch. 26). Taken in the context of the larger narrative, it is one of the most tragic chapters in all Scripture, and at the same time one charged with high hope.

All its elements have their parallels in the Abraham stories: famine, promises from God, disputes over wells, a 'covenant' with Abimelech, the king of Gerar, at Beersheba, and, most remarkably of all, Isaac's telling the men of Gerar that Rebekah, his wife, is his sister. Only the last of these put him in a bad light, but it is enough. He is as intent as his father on saving his own skin, and just as inattentive to the possible consequences for his wife and for the purposes of God. He is manifestly a chip off the old block, and his birth has not, after all, meant a return to the bright world of God's first beginning. The old, familiar order remains in force, and the other parallels in chapter 26 only serve to emphasize the fact. There is the tragedy.

The hope only emerges as the narrative proceeds. God does not begin again. Nor does he desert his world. Indeed a new promise is given Isaac: 'I will be with you' (26.3). After the episode in Gerar it is not rescinded. Instead, when two of Abimelech's envoys come to Isaac at Beersheba, their opening words are, 'We see plainly that the Lord is with you.' God remains committed to the world he has got. The rest of the great narrative, right up to the end of the Books of Kings, and the prophetic books of the Old Testament also, will make clear what this decision costs God, and the Gospels of the New Testament will make it even plainer with their accounts of the passion and death of Jesus of Nazareth.

But the world of chapter 26 is not only familiar to us from the preceding chapters of Genesis. It is familiar to us from our own experience. The ambivalent world of need, high hopes for the future, conflict, disputes, peace-making, and reckless selfishness is the one in which human beings have always lived, and the one in which we find ourselves. It is our world, too, to which God remains so firmly committed. There is the hope.

A life of struggle

If God has problems with Isaac, he has many more with Jacob! Nothing could make clearer the extent of God's commitment to his world than the appearance of the Jacob stories so hard on the heels of those few stories about Isaac.

Jacob's life, as presented in Genesis, is one of struggle and conflict. They begin even before he is born. He struggles with his twin Esau in Rebekah's womb (25.22). The struggle continues in the light of day in two stories which tell how he, the younger brother, gets the better of Esau.

Jacob belongs to a society where a firstborn son is heir to immense and exclusive privileges. All the status, the power, the authority, the prosperity, even the fertility of his father will belong to that son when his father dies. The father, for his part, must make sure that these privileges are properly passed on to him by giving him a death-bed blessing. A younger son must live in the shadow of this fine brother and serve him. From time to time in Ancient Near Eastern literature we find protest made against such conventions. In the Jacob stories there is no explicit complaint, despite the fact that the brothers are twins, born at almost the same moment, and so reveal the unfairness of the privileges particularly clearly. But things are turned topsy-turvy right enough.

The first of the two stories is short and sharp (25.29–34). Esau, the hunter, comes in from the field 'dying of hunger', to find his brother boiling some lentil soup. When he asks to be given some of the soup, Jacob seizes the opportunity, and exchanges a bowl of it for Esau's privileges as the firstborn. The incident is absurd, almost grotesque. As commentators have pointed out, the story provides a case of the slow-witted hunter-gatherer, who is pictured as thinking of nothing but his belly, being smartly out-manoeuvred by the more sophisticated and clever shepherd. It reflects a despising of 'primitive' peoples which is still all too familiar to us. It makes a complete fool out of Esau. 'Thus Esau despised his birthright' is how it ends.

But if we are tempted to share that judgement and the prejudice behind it, the compiler of Genesis would have us think again. After the events of chapter 26 he brings us to the time when Isaac is nearing death, and to the point when the blessing of the eldest son must be given. Isaac proceeds as if he knows nothing of the events surrounding the pot of soup. All must be done with the required ceremony. Rites of passage are like that. They are things of immense significance, and have to be done properly. Esau must prepare a special meal for his father, he must wear his best robes for the occasion. When he comes, his father must formally ask him who he is (the blessing has to be given to the right person). Then the meal will be eaten, the son will kiss his father, and finally the blessing will be pronounced.

The story of this particular blessing begins with the words, '. . . Isaac was old and his eyes were so dim so that he could not see' (27.1). Thus we are told right at the start of Isaac's frailty and vulnerability. We will not be allowed to forget it. All the due ceremonies are performed in their proper order . . . only not with Esau. While he is out hunting, to kill something for his father's meal, Rebekah dresses her favourite son, Jacob, in Esau's clothes, and cooks a meal for him to take to the blessing. She knows that Isaac will take Jacob's hands, and put his hand on his neck when he kisses him. Jacob's skin is much smoother than Esau's, so she puts goatskins on his hands and arms and neck to complete the deception.

The tricks succeed. Isaac is duped, and the blessing pronounced.

> May God give you of the dew of heaven,
> > and of the fatness of the earth,
> > and plenty of grain and wine.
> Let peoples serve you,
> > and nations bow down to you.
> Be lord over your brothers,

and may your mother's sons bow down to you.
Cursed be every one who curses you,
and blessed be every one who blesses you! (27.28–9)

Now Esau's birthright is truly Jacob's. He leaves his father's presence, and almost immediately Esau appears with his meal prepared. The game is up. In a scene of the utmost poignancy we see Isaac's trembling bewilderment turn quickly to horror, and Esau's anguish become murderous hatred of his brother. Isaac is helpless. The blessing cannot be unspoken. He has a blessing to give his eldest and favourite son, but it is a poor thing compared with Jacob's, so poor it is hardly recognizable as a blessing and could be taken for a curse:

Behold away from the fatness of the earth shall your dwelling be,
and away from the dew of heaven on high.
By your sword you shall live,
and you shall serve your brother;
but when you break loose
you shall break his yoke from your neck. (27.39–40)

The story is not written in a didactic style. Mercifully, the storyteller does not preach, nor tell us what to think. But he uses all his very considerable art to make us feel Isaac's and Esau's pain. It does not do him justice to say he is on their side, but he leaves us in no doubt about the horror of what Jacob and Rebekah have done. Rebekah's scheming is as cruel and as ruthless as Sarah's treatment of Hagar and Ishmael. Jacob's taking advantage of his father's blindness and frailty, and his deceiving him at one of the most solemn moments of his life, are reminiscent of the shame and humiliation brought to Noah by his son Ham. Only Jacob's actions are far worse than Ham's, and coldly calculated into the bargain. The rift between the two brothers recalls the one between Cain and Abel and would seem at first to be heading for a similar conclusion. Only when Rebekah learns of Esau's determination to kill his brother, and sends Jacob to her own brother Laban nearly three hundred miles away, is another death of a younger son avoided.

Jacob is a trickster. According to Esau, his very name means deceiver, cheat, one who outwits others (27.36). Outwitting his brother and father was straightforward enough. His uncle Laban is a different proposition altogether. He is a trickster too. The presence of two tricksters on stage at one and the same time is bound to make

for comedy, and so it does here. At one or two points the Jacob/
Laban stories (chs. 29–31) approach bedroom farce. Jacob learns
what it feels like to be cheated himself, even on a wedding night for
which he has waited seven years! Laban puts the wrong daughter of
his in Jacob's bed, and Jacob does not realize it till he wakes up in the
morning! Rebekah sent Jacob to stay with Laban for 'a while'. He
ends up serving Laban for twenty years, in which time he has his
wages changed ten times (and that does not mean continually
increased, either). At the finish of the contest we can just about call
Jacob the victor. Certainly he returns towards the Promised Land in
very different style from the way he left it. He left with nothing. He
returns with two wives, eleven sons and a daughter, male and female
slaves, and large flocks and herds of sheep and goats, camels, cattle
and asses (and Laban's household gods!).

But Jacob's wrestling days are not yet over. His hardest and most
dangerous bouts are still to come.

An encounter on the journey, and preparations for another

When, twenty years before, he fled from Esau's wrath, Jacob
stumbled on a holy place (28.10–22). He lay down to sleep, and had a
vision of a grand stairway linking heaven and earth, its foot at the
very spot where he was lying, and peopled with angels ascending and
descending. In his vision God appeared before him and delivered the
old promises made to Abraham and Isaac. Jacob had wrested a
blessing from his father by a cruel trick. At this holy place, without
any warning, without any cool calculation on his part, he was given a
far richer blessing by God himself. No wonder he woke overcome
with awe: 'Surely the Lord is in this place; and I did not know it . . .
how awesome is this place! This is none other than the house of God,
and this is the gate of heaven.' With the words of the promises
ringing in his ears Jacob crossed the border of the Promised Land,
and continued on his way towards Laban.

Now as he re-enters the Land, he is greeted by angels of God once
more (32.1). God was in exile with him in Laban's country. That the
narrative made quite clear. But he is again in God's Territory, and he
bumps into him again, as the man and the woman bumped into God
in his Garden.

This time the encounter is hurried over. It provides little more
than a footnote to the account of the journey home. It seems to us so
extraordinary, yet the storyteller does not blink an eyelid. Jacob sees

the angels, declares them a company of God's army, and calls the place of his vision Mahanaim. That is all. Has the company appeared to escort him the rest of the way? Certainly it is not hostile to him, for he shows no fear. At Bethel, the place of the vision of the stairway to heaven, God promised him that he would be with him, that he would keep him wherever he went, that he would bring him back to the Land, and would not leave him. God kept his promise in Laban's country. Jacob was keenly aware of that. The vision of God's strength at Mahanaim would seem to come as timely reassurance of his protection in the dangers to come. But if that is how Jacob reads the vision, then God is playing with him. God is the trickster now. It is true that Jacob will emerge more than just unscathed from the danger that fills his mind as he returns home. Esau will pose no threat to him, but will come trailing clouds of forgiveness. But he will meet with another danger on the road, one far greater than he could have imagined, and it will come from God himself.

If Jacob is reassured by the vision at Mahanaim, then the effects soon wear off. Twenty years earlier he fled from an elder brother plotting to kill him. He has no reason to suppose that Esau's feelings have changed. He takes the precautions of sending messengers on ahead, to inform Esau of his return, and to 'find favour' in his sight. The messengers are instructed to tell Esau of Jacob's many possessions, and so to make clear that by 'favour' Jacob does not mean material support. It is not that that he needs, but forgiveness. The precise terms of the message are significant. Jacob calls Esau his 'lord', and himself his 'servant'. This is more than oriental courtesy. It is too far removed from the contempt which he once showed his brother to be simply that. Of course it could be merely the offspring of Jacob's fear. It could be insincere, and betoken an attempt to flatter and manipulate the 'stupid' Esau. Or else it could indicate genuine remorse, and, even more important, an acknowledgement of Esau's status as the elder brother. It could suggest Jacob's willingness to hand Esau back his birthright. The story gives us no clues at this stage. We will have to wait and see.

There is no doubt at all, however, about Jacob's reaction when his messengers return. Esau is coming to meet him with four hundred men. That sounds like war, and Jacob assumes it is. All assurance, all reassurance evaporates. Jacob is 'greatly afraid and distressed'. He has male slaves with him, but they are no fighting force. When eventually he meets Esau, there will be no mention of them, only of the women and children, and the servant girls. Esau was designated a man of war by the terms of Isaac's blessing: 'By your sword you shall live' (27.40). Jacob is in no position to fight him. All he can do is resort to his native cunning and to prayer.

He divides his party and his flocks and herds into two, and plans to put one out of sight of the other. 'If Esau comes to the one company and destroys it, then the company which is left will escape.' Soon he will change those plans, and make them more elaborate.

His prayer is a cry for deliverance from his brother. He addresses God as the God of Abraham and Isaac, the God who has commanded this return to the Land, and who has assured him with the words, 'I will do you good.' He addresses God as the God of the promises, both old and new. He protests he is unworthy (and well he might!) of the love that God has shown him already. 'I am too small for all the steadfast love' (that is a literal translation of the Hebrew, which is much more striking than our English versions) 'and all the faithfulness which thou hast shown to thy servant, for with only my staff I crossed this Jordan; and now I have become two companies.' Thus he acknowledges the source of his prosperity, and claims to be unworthy of the deliverance for which he pleads. He throws himself entirely on the divine generosity of which he has already had such rich experience. 'Deliver me, I pray thee, from the hand of my brother, from the hand of Esau, for I fear him, lest he come and slay us all, the mothers with the children.' There is no attempt to trick or deceive here. Jacob speaks from the heart. It is a fine prayer. The irony of it is this: events will show that he has no need to pray for deliverance from Esau; he needs instead to pray for deliverance from God.

He now abandons the desperate plan of separating his company into two. Instead he keeps his two wives, and their two maids, and the children with him, and divides the rest of the slaves and the animals into *three* parties! These he sends ahead at intervals, having instructed the slaves what to say when Esau comes across them. 'They belong to your servant Jacob; they are a present sent to my lord Esau; and moreover he is behind us.' Together the presents will amount to over 550 animals. They are gifts fit for a king, and so they are meant to be. Jacob cannot approach Esau as a brother. He can only approach him as a vassal might approach a great overlord, a rebellious vassal at that, who now repents his treachery and wishes to make amends. The lengths to which he is prepared to go will become clear when he and Esau meet. For the moment his subservience is emphasized by the repeated talk of 'servant' and 'lord'. If we cannot guess Jacob's motives, the storyteller makes them plain: 'I may appease him with the present that goes before me, and afterwards I shall see his face; perhaps he will accept me.' The Hebrew is again much more colourful than the English. More literally translated that verse runs like this: 'I may cover his face with the present that goes before my face; and afterwards I shall see his face; perhaps he will lift up my face.' By 'covering Esau's face' he means to hide from him his own guilt. The 'lifting up of the face' speaks powerfully and movingly of reconciliation, more so than our grey 'accept' ever can. For good measure there is clearly a play on the word 'face'. The significance of that will become plain at the end of the next passage of the story, one of the strangest and one of the most profound in the entire Bible.

Wrestling with God

Some twenty-five miles north of the Dead Sea a wadi meets the river Jordan from the east, whose stream is called the Jabbok. After the autumn and winter rains the stream becomes a raging torrent, flowing in places along a deep ravine. Jacob has already sent the three droves for his brother on ahead. Now he reaches the Jabbok, and during the night crosses the rest of his entourage over at a ford. Presumably he has remained at the back to supervise the operation. He is left alone in the dark. Now it is his turn to cross. We have been told nothing about the time of year, but for the purposes of the story we must assume that the rains have come, and the waters are high and fast, even though the women and children have got across safely enough.

So far on this journey, except for a moment at Mahanaim, we have been travelling through country we know or can imagine. But at this point the story takes an abrupt turn, and takes us into territory that at first seems quite strange, beyond even our imagining, let alone our experience. Without warning, without any provocation, Jacob is attacked, and 'a man' wrestles with him till the breaking of the day. Since the early years of this century it has been recognized by scholars that this story had its origins in a tale about someone being attacked by the spirit or demon of the Jabbok, the embodiment of the great dangers involved in crossing the river at night after the rains. It stems, therefore, from something primitive and far removed from almost everything else in the Old Testament, with the exception of an even stranger tale in Exodus 4.24–6. Originally it probably had nothing to do with Jacob, but was a local tale told in the region around the Jabbok which somehow found its way into his narrative. It shares many features with other stories found among many peoples: a spirit or evil demon makes a sudden attack on a traveller at night; the traveller is quite unprepared, and the demon means to kill him; nevertheless, in the life and death struggle that ensues the traveller manages to get the upper hand, and before the dawn comes and robs the demon of its power, he extorts from it something of its supernatural strength. Such ancient tales have left traces of themselves behind in fairy stories such as 'The Three Billy-goats Gruff'. The goats are attacked by a troll as they cross a river, and through their cunning and the brute strength of the biggest of them, overcome their assailant and complete the crossing to the lush pasture on the other side.

For a time this story of Jacob at the Jabbok runs true to plot. His attacker is unnamed, mysterious. He is simply 'a man'. That is a clever touch. Knowing stories of hostile spirits as they did, the first hearers of the story would naturally, after gaining a few more of the details, have identified the assailant as the demon of the wadi. The Jacob of the larger Genesis narrative, his mind full of the dangers of his coming encounter with Esau, and thinking that Esau is already on his way to attack him, must naturally assume at first that his attacker is his brother. Both assumptions are wrong. At this point the storyteller is playing the trickster.

The contest is an extraordinary feat of wrestling. It lasts all night. Truly it seems to belong to another world, one where contestants wrestle with supernatural strength and powers of endurance. Yet one of the wrestlers is the all too human Jacob. Perhaps the world we are in is the world of vision, the world of stairways to heaven, and companies of God's army. Or perhaps the plot of a story like this demands such heroism from Jacob, never mind the unheroic qualities he has displayed before. Certainly when Jacob appears to have his assailant in his power, it is precisely what we would expect. The 'man', unable to get the better of Jacob, touches his thigh and puts his hip out of joint. It is dark magic, such as a hostile demon might well display. Yet still Jacob has him in his grip, and the mysterious assailant begs him to let him go 'for the day is breaking'. It was commonly believed that some evil spirits lost their strength in daylight. The 'man's' plea is according to plot, as is Jacob's response, 'I will not let you go, unless you bless me.' The hero must extort something of the demon's power.

Jacob's demand for a blessing is only what we would expect, and yet it prepares us for the turning point in the story, which follows immediately afterwards, and takes us back into the clearer air of the larger narrative. Genesis has spoken a great deal about blessing. The first words spoken by God to creatures of his making in Genesis 1 were words of blessing. The first words spoken by God to Abraham were loud with blessing. The Jacob stories had their beginning in a struggle for blessing, and the power that blessing bestows. It began in Rebekah's womb, continued over a bowl of lentil soup, and finished its first round beside the bed of the dying Isaac. Isaac's blessing was endorsed and enlarged by God in the vision at Bethel. Jacob's talk of blessing invites us to step out of the demon myth and fairy story, back into a land with which we have grown familiar, where human beings bump not into demons, but into God himself.

The assailant's answer to Jacob's demand represents the turning point in the contest, and in the story. Instead of a blessing, he gives a question: 'What is your name?' Blessings cannot be extorted here, even though the dawn has not quite arrived. For the first time in the contest since the initial attack, Jacob's adversary seizes the initiative. Though still in Jacob's grip, he is not to be ordered about.

Yet in another respect the story would seem to be running still true to plot. In many stories of contests such as these, each contestant struggles to learn the identity of the other. He who has the name of the other will have him in his power. All the more surprising then that Jacob should at once comply and give his name, but that is what he does. The response of the attacker is, however, much more astonishing still: 'Your name shall no more be called Jacob, but Israel, for you have striven with God' (or is it 'gods'?) 'and with men, and have prevailed.' (The name 'Israel' is here understood as coming from a rare Hebrew verb meaning 'strive' or 'exert oneself'. In fact, we cannot be sure what it really means.)

There is a telling ambiguity in the Hebrew here, as if the attacker is playing with Jacob, and the storyteller with us. The word translated 'God' is plural in form, and though in the vast majority of its occurrences in the Old Testament it means 'God', it can equally well mean 'gods', or 'divine or supernatural beings', including river demons and evil spirits of the night. It could confirm, therefore, any suspicion we and Jacob may have that the wrestling match is with the demon of the Jabbok. Alternatively, understood as 'gods-and-men' the phrase could simply be a figure of speech. It occurs as that in Judges 9.9 and 13, and here it might indicate nothing more than the all-embracing nature of the struggles which Jacob has engaged in during the course of his life. It might signify hardly anything at all.

Yet with these same teasing words Jacob is given a new name, a new identity. When he told his assailant his name, he told him that he was a deceiver, a cheat, one who outwits others and extorts blessings from them. That is what the name Jacob means, as we have seen. But he cannot extort blessings here. He cannot be a trickster now. Instead he must wear the name and identity of the future people of God, those who struggle with men and with God. For surely in the end it must be God. He it was who turned Abram into Abraham (17.5), and Sarai into Sarah (17.15), and who gave Isaac his name before he was born (17.19). He it is with whom his people will indeed wrestle. On the other side of the argument it is inconceivable that the ancestor of the people of God, and through him that nation itself, should receive their name from a local demon of an insignificant wadi.

It must be God. Suspicion grows in Jacob's mind. 'Tell me, I pray, your name,' he asks. Given what we now know, this is much more than the expected attempt to find out a demon's identity, though it sounds very like it. Jacob is not dealing with a demon, and when the answer to his question comes, together with the dawn, he knows that himself for certain: ' "Why is it that you ask my name?" And there he blessed him. So Jacob called the name of the place Peniel,' (which means in Hebrew 'The Face of God') 'saying, "For I have seen God face to face, and yet my life is preserved." ' 'The wrestling match is over, the assailant disappears, and the sun rises upon Jacob as he leaves Peniel, limping because of the injury to his hip.

The encounter at Bethel ended with words of blessing, with the coming of the dawn, and with recognition. 'Then Jacob awoke from his sleep and said, "Surely the Lord is in this place; and I did not know it" ' (28.16). The act of blessing and the dawn brought him then to his physical and spiritual senses. So too now at Peniel. The blessing at Bethel was given against all deserving. So undeserving of it was Jacob, that we might have accused God then of arbitrary favour, worse, of siding with the oppressor instead of the oppressed, as once he seemed to side with Sarah and Abraham against Hagar and Ishmael. But that is the way of God's blessing. His generosity does not abide by our rules. He throws his largesse to all and sundry. His blessing always comes as a surprise, and can be recognized by its very 'arbitrariness' and seeming absurdity. This abiding feature of

God's mischief got a certain Jesus of Nazareth into deep trouble, for he was that same generosity incarnate. At Peniel the blessing runs true to form. It is not given when it is demanded. Generosity cannot be shown on demand, for then it is not generosity. The blessing is given when Jacob, and we, the hearers of the story, least expect it. Given like that it is instantly recognizable.

Now, at last, Jacob realizes the full extent of the danger he has been in all night. 'I have seen God face to face, and yet my life is preserved.' The words remind us of Hagar's cry, when she was first driven into the desert and rescued by God: 'Have I really seen God and remained alive after seeing him?' (16.13). When dealing with the story of God's Garden, we remarked upon the danger which the ancient Israelites associated with holy things. But if objects to do with God could be regarded as so dangerous, how much more God himself! Even Moses, when he asked to see God's glory, was told, 'You cannot see my face; for man shall not see me and live' (Exod. 33.20). Jacob thought at first, perhaps, that he was wrestling with a brother intent on killing him and getting his revenge. Next, surely, he must have thought he was up against a demon intent on destroying him for no reason at all. In truth, as he now knows, he has been fighting with a God intent on blessing for a reason hidden in his deep purposes of redemption. Well might he be bewildered, and go on his way limping. In the next stage of his journey he will meet again with unexpected magnanimity.

Making sense of God for a second time

But we cannot move on to his meeting with Esau quite yet. We must stop, as we stopped at the end of the story of the binding of Isaac, that other story about God bringing a bearer of his promises to the brink of death, and ask more about what has been going on. We suggested with Genesis 22 that certain aspects of its theology could not be pushed very far, that theological caution had been sacrificed in the interests of storytelling. That would seem to be the case here, where we must remember that the storyteller had as his raw material a tale about a demon far, far removed from the mainstream of Israel's talk about her God. Yet we must be careful not to use these observations as an excuse to disregard those features of the story which do not immediately appeal, or which immediately appal. If we do ignore them, we may find we have thrown the baby out with the bath water.

The notion of God attacking someone without provocation might well seem horrendous, and quite alien to any theology of the Cross. It is not, however, entirely alien to religious experience. The Old Testament bears frequent witness to Israel's sense of being under attack from her God, and being brought by him to the verge of extinction. We Christians might want to interpret things differently, yet in his masterpiece, 'The Wreck of the Deutschland', the Jesuit nineteenth-century poet, Gerard Manley Hopkins, found himself writing these lines:

> I did say yes
> O at lightning and lashed rod;
> Thou heardst me truer than tongue confess
> Thy terror, O Christ, O God;
> Thou knowest the walls, altar and hour and night:
> The swoon of a heart that the sweep and the hurl of thee trod
> Hard down with a horror of height:
> And the midriff astrain with leaning of, laced with fire of stress.

Hopkins and Jacob would have understood one another.

Secondly, we might think it daring in the extreme, if not plain wrong, that the storyteller should represent God as being in Jacob's grip until nearly the end of the contest. The picture of God at a man's mercy is surely one derived from the story's primitive origins, and no longer to be taken seriously. But if that is our conclusion, then we miss perhaps the most profound contribution this story has to make to theology and to faith. Are we not presented in the stories of Christ's passion and crucifixion with a picture of God at men's (and it is *men's*, not women's) mercy? And since the blindness and brutality recorded in those accounts has in no wise disappeared from human society, have we not a crucified God still? Tragically the story of God's wrestling match makes all too good sense, and a tale which bears so clearly the marks of its primitive beginnings can take us to the very summit of Calvary, and deep into the still broken heart of God.

A reunion and a parting

After the heroics of the binding of Isaac came comedy and a hero made into a fool. After Peniel, when for a night Jacob also, so unheroic hitherto, played a hero's part, we are given more subtle comedy and another hero brought down to earth. Such is still the mischief and the sure grasp of reality of the compiler of Genesis. But the account of the meeting of Esau and Jacob goes deeper than the story of the purchase of Sarah's burial plot. There is pathos to be found in it in abundance, and images of love and great nobility of spirit. It shows something of the best that human beings are capable of, and hints too of their tragic failure to grasp that best and hold on to it. And it provokes disturbing theological questions.

One of the most remarkable things about the Peniel story is that the larger narrative proceeds almost entirely as if it was not there. Even the new name of Israel is not used for some time (it reappears in 35.10 and thereafter in Genesis is used interchangeably with Jacob). It is not enough to say that the compiler has inserted a story that once had a quite independent existence. That is to explain why it is not picked up in the narrative, but it does not explore the more significant matter of the effect of what the compiler has done.

The immediate effect is marvellous irony. The three droves sent on as presents to Esau have reached him, and now Esau and his four hundred men are within sight of Jacob and his little entourage. Jacob divides his party into three groups, putting the slave women with their children in front, his wife Leah with her children next, and his favourite wife Rachel with her son Joseph last. Then he goes forward, as he must, to meet Esau himself, 'bowing himself to the ground seven times' as he goes. This is court ceremonial. We commented earlier that his gifts for Esau were fit for a king, and such as a rebellious vassal might offer as a sign of his remorse and willingness to return to obedience. His actions now speak the same language. When God appeared to Abraham in the guise of three strangers in need of hospitality, Abraham greeted them by bowing himself to the ground once (18.2). When two angels, again in disguise, met Lot in Sodom, he also welcomed them by bowing to the ground once (19.1). Here, when Jacob meets his own brother, he meets him with all the courtly ceremony with which petty vassal princes used to greet their Pharaoh. He, Jacob, who has wrestled with God all night and has more than survived the experience, now grovels before his brother! It is comic. The compiler rubs the nose of the hero of Peniel in the dust . . . seven times! It is tragic, also. Jacob's action betokens great fear, and declares louder than any words the rift that he feels must lie between him and Esau. At the same time it has remorse about it and generosity of spirit. Jacob's

ceremonies must surely express his subservience to his brother, as
we thought his language of 'lord' and 'servant' might possibly have
done earlier. No longer does he cling on to the status that he wrested
from him with such arrogance and cruelty. He hands Esau back his
birthright, and soon he will make that clear in words, or, to be more
precise, in a word.

But his elaborate ceremonies are also quite unnecessary, and quite
misplaced. Esau does not come for revenge, but out of love. Showing
none of the great dignity of a Pharaoh, he runs to meet Jacob,
embraces him, falls on his neck and kisses him. He does precisely
what the father will do when his younger son returns in Jesus's
parable of 'The Prodigal Son' (indeed the whole of that parable finds
its basis in the Jacob/Esau stories). No wonder the brothers fall to
weeping. Reunion as charged with forgiveness as this must make for
tears.

The women and children now catch up their master, and each
group in turn bows down before Esau. At least they do not perform
Jacob's absurd pantomine of prostrating themselves seven times.
They simply show the courtesy and respect demanded of them in
such a society as theirs. Nevertheless, their formality sits ill at ease
with Esau's spontaneous show of love. Jacob reveals by his first
words to Esau that he belongs still to the world of their stiff courtesy,
and not yet to that of his brother's gay abandon. To Esau's asking
who the women and children are, he replies, 'The children whom
God has graciously given your servant.' Still 'your servant'. But if
that disappoints us, the rest of his reply should not.

When Esau next asks him about the purpose of the three droves
sent on ahead (it would appear that the slaves accompanying them
have not passed on Jacob's message), Jacob answers, 'To find favour
in the sight of my lord.' Still the disappointment of 'my lord', but
that is balanced by a profound play on words. The Hebrew word
translated 'graciously given' in Jacob's first answer is *ḥanan*. The
word translated 'favour' in the second is *ḥen*. The second word is the
noun formed from the first word, the verb. They speak of grace,
compassion, forgiveness. Jacob ha discovered the grace, compassion and forgiveness of God. His family are for him living proof of
them. Now he hopes to find the same favour in the eyes of his
brother.

He is not let down. Esau protests that he has no need of Jacob's
gifts: 'I have enough, my brother; keep what you have for yourself.'
This is a more generous protest even than it seems at first sight, for

Jacob's possessions include Esau's birthright, and Isaac's blessing that had been meant for him. Esau may be rich and powerful (he has four hundred men with him after all), and undoubtedly he means just what he says. But the extent of his magnanimity cannot fail to astonish, and indeed it is not lost on Jacob. In pressing Esau further to accept his gifts, he declares, ' . . . for truly to see your face is like seeing the face of God, so kindly have you received me.' 'I have seen God face to face, and yet my life is preserved' were his words at the start of the day. Here and here only the storyteller glances back to the contest at Peniel. That contest began with great fear, and ended with mercy never dreamed of before. For Jacob reunion with his brother has begun and ended in the same way. Now we, the readers of the narrative, know why the compiler put the story of Peniel exactly where he did, and have had another glimpse of his genius.

Jacob must insist that Esau receives his gifts, because of what they represent. In case Esau has not yet got the message, he says to him, 'Accept, I pray you, my gift that is brought to you,' and he uses a new word for gift, *berakah*. *Berakah* can indeed mean 'gift' or 'present', but its usual meaning is 'blessing'. It is the word we have heard so often in Genesis. It is the word which came up time and again in the story of Jacob's tricking his dying father. Now the truth is plain for all to see, including Esau. Jacob was not expecting forgiveness from his brother. Esau cannot have been expecting such remorse, such willingness to make amends from Jacob. Such things cannot be scorned, and Esau is in no mood for scorn anyway. He takes his blessing back.

The reconciliation is complete, or so Esau supposes. But Jacob still does not belong to his world. To Esau the reunion means they must now journey on together, but when he suggests it Jacob replies: 'My lord knows that the children are frail, and that the flocks and herds giving suck are a care to me; and if they are overdriven for one day, all the flocks will die. Let my lord pass on before his servant, and I will lead on slowly, according to the pace of the cattle which are before me and according to the pace of the children, until I come to my lord in Seir.' Jacob was able to return the blessing he stole. But it is not in his power to give back the blessings and the promises given by God. The land of Canaan is promised to him and his descendants, but not to Esau. Esau lives in the land of Seir to the south of the Dead Sea. Jacob must follow the lead of the promises, and their ways must part. He has no intention of following Esau to Seir, as he reveals when he leaves his brother and travels on towards the west. His

courtesy demands that he is less than candid. He cannot turn down
Esau's suggestion flat. He must pretend he means to catch him up.

Yet the terms of his pretence are heavy with tragedy. His whole
speech is still dictated by the formality with which he began. Only
his tears spoke of brotherly love. For the rest he has persisted in
wearing the guise of a vassal before his overlord. Earlier we might
have said his conduct and manner of speech were appropriate for one
who wished to renounce the status he had stolen, and show his
recognition of Esau's authority as the elder son. But now that the
truth is out on both sides, they are surely singularly out of place. It is
not just that he persists in the language of 'lord' and 'servant' when
Esau has called him 'brother', though that is significant enough. The
whole pretence about his future plans does not belong to relations
between brothers, especially brothers who have just wept on each
other's shoulders, and who have shown each other such surprising
willingness for reunion. Furthermore, the excuses he makes smack
of the old trickery. Esau, with all the animals Jacob has given him,
can hardly proceed at a mad gallop. As for Jacob's animals, surely
they will not die if they are driven too fast for *one* day. His assertion is
absurd. Esau does not quibble. He makes one final offer, to leave
some of his men behind to escort Jacob and his party on their way.
This too is rejected: 'What need is there? Let me find favour in the
sight of my lord.' (As if he has not found favour enough already!)
This final courtesy also is utterly misplaced. Esau has no further
answer to make. He goes on his way to Seir, and very nearly leaves
the narrative altogether. He will meet Jacob again, at Isaac's burial
(35.29), and chapter 36 is devoted to him and to lists of his
descendants. That chapter notes briefly that he and Jacob agreed to
part because the land would not support all their flocks and herds
and allow them to live together. This clearly originated as an
independent account of their separation. Still it is now part of the
larger narrative, and read as that it suggests a period of peaceful co-
existence before their final parting. After that the narrative has time
only for Jacob.

A scandal of particularity

But that is not the end of the story for Esau. Genesis 36 reminds its
readers that Esau was the ancestor of the Edomites. For hundreds of
years Israel and Edom were sworn enemies. According to Kings,
David waged a six-month campaign against Edom, in which he

attempted the slaughter of all adult males (1 Kings 11.15–17). When Judah was devastated by the Babylonians at the start of the sixth century BCE, the Edomites shared with the Babylonians in the capture and looting of Jerusalem, handed survivors over to them, and caught many trying to escape (Obad. 10–14). With many of Judah's people exiled to Babylonia, the Edomites took further advantage of the situation, moved into the southern part of the country, and established their own capital at Hebron. Obadiah and Psalm 137 bear eloquent witness to the bitterness these actions caused. The Edomites' new territory became known as Idumaea. In the second century BCE Judas Maccabaeus led sorties into Idumaea in revenge for attacks on Jews, and later in the same century John Hyrcanus conquered the territory, and forced the Idumaeans to accept circumcision and obedience to the Jewish Law. The Herods of Jesus' time and before were Idumaeans, and that accounts partly for why so many Jews despised and hated their rule.

As a result of all this Esau's name became blackened among the Jews. He and Edom were synonymous. Within the Old Testament itself we can see the beginnings of a move to exalt Jacob and damn his brother. 'I have loved Jacob,' says the God of Malachi (1.2–3; Malachi was probably written in the first half of the fifth century BCE), 'but I have hated Esau.' Beyond the Old Testament, in the second century BCE *Book of Jubilees*, Jacob is turned into a blameless, upright figure, and, dare we say it, an utter prig of a man, while Esau is a villain through and through. The story of their reunion is hurried across. Four hundred years later some rabbis even managed to turn Esau's running to meet his brother to his discredit. According to them he did not kiss Jacob, but bit him on the neck!

The storytellers and the compiler of Genesis will have almost none of this. Though some of the writing and most if not all the compilation were done not so long after the notorious events surrounding the capture of Jerusalem in 587 or 586, only in the little story of the bowl of lentil soup is Esau portrayed in a poor light. In chapter 33 he is a noble figure of godlike magnanimity. In chapter 27, when Jacob steals his blessing, the writer goes to great lengths, as we have indicated already, to evoke our sympathy for Esau, and to help us share his anguish. He does nothing to hide or excuse Jacob's cruelty.

Yet a great diffculty, if not a scandal remains. Some years ago Christian theologians coined the phrase 'the scandal of particularity' to refer to the apparent problems surrounding the identification of a particular, historical individual with the Son of God. We have a 'scandal of particularity' of a different kind in Genesis, the scandal of God's choosing one and not another. When we were dealing with the blessings Jacob received at Bethel and at Peniel, we spoke of God throwing his largesse 'to all and sundry'. In truth that phrase does not quite fit the Jacob/Esau narratives. The divine promises are made to Jacob and *not* to Esau. Jacob is the one who with his descendants is destined for God's land, while Esau must turn aside for Seir. Admittedly, it is not true to say that Esau is not blessed by God. The wealth and power he clearly possesses by the time he is reunited with his brother would have been regarded by the writer and the first hearers of the story as clear signs of God's blessing. Still it remains that there is no equivalent for Esau of the fine blessings received by Jacob at Bethel and Peniel. Beside the bed of the dying Isaac Esau was excluded, denied, humiliated. By the time he leaves the narrative the humiliation has gone, but the exclusion remains. He remains a bystander on the edge of God's purposes, and one who has suffered grievously that those purposes might go forward. Ironically those same purposes include, as we have seen, the re-creation of a world where such exclusion is not to be found, but instead there is harmony, joy, and a universal sense of belonging and being at home. At the beginning of Genesis that was well understood. With the Jacob/Esau narratives we begin to see it being lost sight of, though the descriptions of Jacob's cruelty and deceitfulness, and the contrast made with Esau's generosity, make us think the compiler was protesting against the direction in which his material was leading him. As the narrative proceeds beyond Genesis, and becomes enmeshed in the story of the fortunes not of Israel the patriarch, but of Israel the people of God, it will prove much harder for the writers and compilers to keep the original purposes in view. At times they will get trampled into the ground. We will see that happen on the site of Jericho in our fifth chapter. In the end it will need the writer of Jonah to recall the great truth which his people found, and which the Church still finds so hard to grasp, namely that God does indeed throw his largesse to *all* and sundry.

4

TWO GIFTS OF MANNA AND QUAILS. Why does Sinai make such a difference?

(Exodus 16, Numbers 11)

Matters of life and death: the passages compared

Our approach in this chapter must be rather different. In each chapter so far the passages chosen for detailed comment have been consecutive. We have been concerned with how one leads into the other, or how the second strikes sparks off the first. Here our passages are widely separated from one another, yet parallel each other. Our task will be one of comparing and contrasting them. In the last two chapters we took some time to reach the chosen texts. This time, after setting the passages in their context in the briefest possible way, we will turn to them straight away. Our discoveries about their similarities and differences will lead us to examine other passages in Exodus and Numbers, and our desire to explain certain features of all these texts will then encourage us to look at the positions they occupy in the larger narrative, and so discuss their contexts in greater detail. Thus we will arrive at the context from the passages rather than the passages from the context.

Though Abraham receives the promise of the land of Canaan in Genesis 12 and, by God's terms, takes possession of it in the next chapter, his descendants do not enter it as a people until the book of Joshua, and the business of conquest is not finished till David is secure on the throne half-way through the second Book of Samuel. In between promise and entry lie not only the stories of Isaac and Jacob, but the long story of Joseph and the other sons of Jacob, a period of 430 years spent in Egypt by their descendants, most of it in slave labour, a dramatic escape from the Pharaoh and his army, and forty years of wandering or living in the wilderness of the Sinai peninsula. Exodus 16 and Numbers 11 both belong to that last stage of the wilderness. They belong to a point (if three-and-a-half books can be called a point, for it lasts from half-way through Exodus to the end of Deuteronomy) of great tension in the narrative. The promise to Abraham of a son has been fulfilled; his descendants have indeed become multiplied 'as the stars of heaven and as the sand which is on the sea shore' (Gen 22.17). Now we await the entry into the Promised Land, the turning of the people into an independent nation of some renown (you will remember that was the vision implied by the terms of the promises made at the start of Genesis 12), and their becoming a source of blessing for 'all the families of the earth'. Our chosen passages speak of the time between fulfilment and fulfilment. In more senses than one they belong to no man's land.

In order to compare them more easily, we will set them out side by side, using the text of the RSV. There is one complication. Numbers 11 is a conflation of two stories which in Exodus are treated quite separately. The story of the manna and the quails is combined with an account of Moses sharing some of his power and his duties with seventy of the elders of the people. The second story does not find its parallel in Exodus till chapter 18. We cannot simply remove it from Numbers 11 and put it aside, for it has been too closely intertwined with the giving of manna and quails. Nor would we wish to ignore it if we could, for its relation to its counterpart in Exodus is both interesting and significant. We have therefore appended the text of the relevant part of Exodus 18 to that of chapter 16.

Exodus 16	Numbers 11
1 They set out from Elim, and all the congregation of the people of Israel came to the wilderness of Sin, which is between Elim and Sinai, on the fifteenth day of the second month after they had departed from the land of Egypt. ²And the whole congregation of the people of Israel	1 And the people complained in the hearing of the LORD about their misfortunes; and when the LORD heard it, his anger was kindled, and the fire of the LORD burned among them, and consumed some outlying parts of the camp.² Then the people cried to Moses; and Moses prayed to

murmured against Moses and Aaron in the wilderness,[3] and said to them, 'Would that we had died by the hand of the LORD in the land of Egypt, when we sat by the fleshpots and ate bread to the full; for you have brought us out into this wilderness to kill this whole assembly with hunger.'

4 Then the LORD said to Moses, 'Behold, I will rain bread from heaven for you; and the people shall go out and gather a day's portion every day, that I may prove them, whether they will walk in my law or not. [5]On the sixth day, when they prepare what they bring in, it will be twice as much as they gather daily.' [6]So Moses and Aaron said to all the people of Israel, 'At evening you shall know that it was the LORD who brought you out of the land of Egypt, [7]and in the morning you shall see the glory of the LORD, because he has heard your murmurings against the LORD. For what are we, that you murmur against us?' [8]And Moses said, 'When the LORD gives you in the evening flesh to eat and in the morning bread to the full, because the LORD has heard your murmurings which you murmur against him – what are we? Your murmurings are not against us but against the LORD.'

9 And Moses said to Aaron, 'Say to the whole congregation of the people of Israel, "Come near before the LORD, for he has heard your murmurings." ' [10]And as Aaron spoke to the whole congregation of the people of Israel they looked toward the wilderness, and behold, the glory of the LORD appeared in the cloud. [11]And the LORD said to Moses, [12]'I have heard the murmurings of the people of Israel; say to them, "At twilight you shall eat flesh, and in the morning you shall

the LORD, and the fire abated. [3]So the name of that place was called Tabérah, because the fire of the LORD burned among them.

4 Now the rabble that was among them had a strong craving; and the people of Israel also wept again, and said, 'O that we had meat to eat! [5]We remember the fish we ate in Egypt for nothing, the cucumbers, the melons, the leeks, the onions, and the garlic; [6]but now our strength is dried up, and there is nothing at all but this manna to look at.'

7 Now the manna was like coriander seed, and its appearance like that of bdellium. [8]The people went about and gathered it, and ground it in mills or beat it in mortars, and boiled it in pots, and made cakes of it; and the taste of it was like the taste of cakes baked with oil.[9] When the dew fell upon the camp in the night, the manna fell with it.

10 Moses heard the people weeping throughout their families, every man at the door of his tent; and the anger of the LORD blazed hotly, and Moses was displeased. [11]Moses said to the LORD, 'Why hast thou dealt ill with thy servant? And why have I not found favour in thy sight, that thou dost lay the burden of all this people upon me? [12]Did I conceive all this people? Did I bring them forth, that thou shouldst say to me, "Carry them in your bosom, as a nurse carries the sucking child, to the land which thou didst swear to give their fathers?" [13]Where am I to get meat to give to all this people? For they weep before me and say, "Give us meat, that we may eat."[14] I am not able to carry all this people alone, the burden is too heavy for me. [15]If thou wilt deal thus with me, kill me at once, if I find favour in thy

be filled with bread; then you shall know that I am the LORD your God." '

13 In the evening quails came up and covered the camp; and in the morning dew lay round about the camp. [14]And when the dew had gone up, there was on the face of the wilderness a fine, flake-like thing, fine as hoarfrost on the ground. [15]When the people of Israel saw it, they said to one another, 'What is it?' For they did not know what it was. And Moses said to them, 'It is the bread which the LORD has given you to eat. [16] This is what the LORD has commanded: "Gather of it, every man of you, as much as he can eat; you shall take an omer apiece, according to the number of the persons whom each of you has in his tent." ' [17]And the people of Israel did so; they gathered, some more, some less. [18]But when they measured it with an omer, he that gathered much had nothing over, and he that gathered little had no lack; each gathered according to what he could eat. [19]And Moses said to them, 'Let no man leave any of it till the morning.' [20] But they did not listen to Moses; some left part of it till the morning, and it bred worms and became foul; and Moses was angry with them. [21]Morning by morning they gathered it, each as much as he could eat; but when the sun grew hot, it melted.

22 On the sixth day they gathered twice as much bread, two omers apiece; and when all the leaders of the congregation came and told Moses, [23]he said to them, 'This is what the LORD has commanded: "Tomorrow is a day of solemn rest, a holy sabbath to the LORD; bake what you will bake and boil what you will boil, and all that is left over lay by to be kept till the morning." ' [24]So they laid it by till

sight, that I may not see my wretchedness.'

16 And the LORD said to Moses, 'Gather for me seventy men of the elders of Israel, whom you know to be the elders of the people and officers over them; and bring them to the tent of meeting, and let them take their stand there with you. [17]And I will come down and talk with you there; and I will take some of the spirit which is upon you and put it upon them; and they shall bear the burden of the people with you, that you may not bear it yourself alone. [18]And say to the people, "Consecrate yourselves for tomorrow, and you shall eat meat; for you have wept in the hearing of the LORD, saying, 'Who will give us meat to eat? For it was well with us in Egypt.' Therefore the LORD will give you meat, and you shall eat. [19]You shall not eat one day, or two days, or five days, or ten days, or twenty days, [20]but a whole month, until it comes out at your nostrils and becomes loathsome to you, because you have rejected the LORD who is among you, and have wept before him, saying, 'Why did we come forth out of Egypt?' " ' [21]But Moses said, 'The people among whom I am number six hundred thousand on foot; and thou hast said, "I will give them meat, that they may eat a whole month!" [22]Shall flocks and herds be slaughtered for them, to suffice them? Or shall all the fish of the sea be gathered together for them, to suffice them?' [23]And the LORD said to Moses, 'Is the LORD's hand shortened? Now you shall see whether my word will come true for you or not.'

24 So Moses went out and told the people the words of the LORD; and he gathered seventy men of the elders of the people, and placed

the morning, as Moses bade them; and it did not become foul, and there were no worms in it. [25]Moses said, 'Eat it today, for today is a sabbath to the LORD; today you will not find it in the field.[26] Six days you shall gather it; but on the seventh day, which is a sabbath, there will be none.' [27]On the seventh day some of the people went out to gather and they found none. [28]And the LORD said to Moses, 'How long do you refuse to keep my commandments and my laws? [29]See! The LORD has given you the sabbath, therefore on the sixth day he gives you bread for two days; remain every man of you in his place, let no man go out of his place on the seventh day.' [30]So the people rested on the seventh day.

31 Now the house of Israel called its name manna; it was like coriander seed, white, and the taste of it was like wafers made with honey. [32]And Moses said, 'This is what the LORD has commanded: "Let an omer of it be kept throughout your generations, that they may see the bread with which I fed you in the wilderness, when I brought you out of the land of Egypt." ' [33]And Moses said to Aaron, 'Take a jar, and put an omer of manna in it, and place it before the LORD, to be kept throughout your generations.' [34]As the LORD commanded Moses, so Aaron placed it before the testimony, to be kept. [35]And the people of Israel ate the manna forty years, till they came to a habitable land; they ate the manna, till they came to the border of the land of Canaan. [36](An omer is the tenth part of an ephah.)

Exodus 18.13–27

13 On the morrow Moses sat to judge the people, and the people them round about the tent. [25]Then the LORD came down in the cloud and spoke to him, and took some of the spirit that was upon him and put it upon the seventy elders; and when the spirit rested upon them, they prophesied. But they did so no more.

26 Now two men remained in the camp, one named Eldad, and the other named Medad, and the spirit rested upon them; they were among those registered, but they had not gone out to the tent, and so they prophesied in the camp. [27]And a young man ran and told Moses, 'Eldad and Medad are prophesying in the camp.' [28]And Joshua the son of Nun, the minister of Moses, one of his chosen men, said, 'My lord Moses, forbid them.' [29]But Moses said to him, 'Are you jealous for my sake? Would that all the LORD's people were prophets, that the LORD would put his spirit upon them!' [30]And Moses and the elders of Israel returned to the camp.

31 And there went forth a wind from the LORD, and it brought quails from the sea, and let them fall beside the camp, about a day's journey on this side and a day's journey on the other side, round about the camp, and about two cubits above the face of the earth. [32]And the people rose all that day, and all night, and all the next day, and gathered the quails; he who gathered least gathered ten homers; and they spread them out for themselves all around the camp. [33]While the meat was yet between their teeth, before it was consumed, the anger of the LORD was kindled against the people, and the LORD smote the people with a very great plague. [34]Therefore the name of that place was called Kib´roth-hatta´avah,

stood about Moses from morning till evening. [14]When Moses' father-in-law saw all that he was doing for the people, he said, 'What is this that you are doing for the people? Why do you sit alone, and all the people stand about you from morning till evening?' [15]And Moses said to his father-in-law, 'Because the people come to me to inquire of God: [16]when they have a dispute, they come to me and I decide between a man and his neighbour, and I make them know the statutes of God and his decisions.' [17]Moses' father-in-law said to him, 'What you are doing is not good. [18]You and the people with you will wear yourselves out for the thing is too heavy for you, you are not able to perform it alone. [19]Listen now to my voice; I will give you counsel, and God be with you! You shall represent the people before God, and bring their cases to God; [20]and you shall teach them the statutes and the decisions, and make them know the way in which they must walk and what they must do. [21]Moreover choose able men from all the people, such as fear God, men who are trustworthy and who hate a bribe; and place such men over the people as rulers of thousands, of hundreds, of fifties, and of tens. [22]And let them judge the people at all times; every great matter they shall bring to you but any small matter they shall decide themselves; so it will be easier for you, and they will bear the burden with you. [23]If you do this, and God so commands you, then you will be able to endure, and all this people also will go to their place in peace.'

24 So Moses gave heed to the voice of his father-in-law and did all that he had said. [25]Moses chose able men out of all Israel, and made them heads over the people, rulers of because there they buried the people who had the craving. [35]From Kib'-roth-hatta'avah the people journeyed to Haze'roth; and they remained at Haze'roth.

thousands, of hundreds, of fifties, and of tens. [26]And they judged the people at all times; hard cases they brought to Moses, but any small matter they decided themselves. [27]Then Moses let his father-in-law depart, and he went his way to his own country.

Both passages begin with need and with complaint. The need is real, or certainly felt to be real, and the complaints are understandable. The desert of the Sinai peninula as it is painted in the narrative is a harsh place. Some know how to live in such deserts, and meet their terrible demands. They know because they have always lived in deserts, and their parents and grandparents before them. The desert was new to Israel. Furthermore, they had come into it straight from slavery. They had been born into slavery, and their parents and grandparents before them. They were not used to exercising responsibility for themselves. They were used to obeying orders. If their bodies had not been quite crushed to death by the labours they had been forced to perform for their Egyptian taskmasters, then surely their spirits had been. Those who have tried it know how hard it is to liberate the oppressed. Subservience becomes a habit, and to step outside it is indeed a going out into the unknown, a going into a wilderness, where there are no clear paths forward, where life is precarious, and survival itself uncertain.

Yet in both passages the complaints are clearly meant to be regarded as reprehensible. It would seem hard to know where the greater fault is to be found. In Exodus the people's need is extreme. They see themselves faced with starvation. They have nothing at all to eat. In Numbers starvation is not the problem, but monotony of diet. The manna has already been given. They have their regular supply. But they have nothing else. The taste of manna has gone sour on them. The complaints in Numbers would seem less justifiable than those in Exodus. Yet the terms of the complaints in Exodus are terrible. The chapters preceding this one tell of the Passover and the miracle at the Reed Sea. They tell of how God killed in a night all the firstborn sons of the Egyptians, and spared those of his own people. They tell of how the Israelites were caught between the Reed Sea and the pursuing Egyptian army, and how God drove the Egyptians into the sea to drown, while leading his people across to safety.

> I will sing to the Lord, for he has triumphed gloriously;
>> the horse and the rider he has thrown into the sea.
> The Lord is my strength and my song,
>> and he has become my salvation;
> this is my God, and I will praise him,
>> my father's God, and I will exalt him. (Exod.15.1–2)

That is how the people began their great song of triumph after the crossing of the sea. The event went down in their traditions as the greatest act of salvation ever performed by their God on their behalf. It came to occupy the seat of highest honour in their gospel. But here they are, at the start of chapter 16, wishing aloud that God had not passed them by on that dreadful night in Egypt, *accusing* Moses, accusing *Moses*, of bringing them into the desert to die! The grand symphony of the song has turned so quickly into a raucous and bitter cacophony, drowning all sound of the truth. They rub salt into God's wounds by romanticizing about the past. The story does not tell us what the Israelites had to eat in Egypt, but it gives our imaginations enough information to work on. We hear of forced and hard labour, of beatings and groanings, of attempts to have all male children born to the slave women put to death at birth, of the screw being given yet another turn and the people being worked to near-exhaustion. It is a tale of naked oppression, and there are many in the world who still recognize it as their own. We hear also of a series of disasters visited by God on the country, in order to force the Egyptians' hands. In passages written not without humour, though theirs is the blackest of black comedy, we read of the water of the Nile turned to blood, of plagues of frogs, gnats, flies, and locusts, of the domestic animals of the Egyptians dying of disease, of a terrible outbreak of boils, of death-dealing hailstorms, and an awesome and fearful darkness. All this, and then the killing of the Egyptian firstborn. Sometimes it is made plain that the Israelites were not directly affected by these disasters, but we have to say that this particular Egypt hardly sounds the sort of place to romanticize about! The Israelites' complaints are shocking, and ridiculous.

In Numbers 11 we find the same looking back to Egypt through rose-coloured spectacles. Beyond that very little. Only the longing for meat (some commentators have called it a lust, but the Hebrew does not pass that judgement), the claim that their appetite is gone, or their throats are dry, or, as the RSV has it, their strength is dried up (the Hebrew will sustain all those translations), and an unspecified

complaining about their misfortunes. Admittedly, this last complaint, made at the very start of the chapter, is harsher than it
sounds. In 10.29 Moses invited his father-in-law to accompany them
on their journeyings with the words, ' . . . come with us, and we will
do you good; for the Lord has promised good to Israel.' The word
used for 'misfortunes' in 11.1 is the usual Hebrew term for evil. In
such a context it speaks plainly of the blindness of the people, and
their preoccupation with the needs of the moment. While Moses
looks forward to the 'good' to come, their minds are fixed on the
'evil' of the present.

If we try to weigh up the two sets of complaints, bearing in mind
the greater need of the people in the Exodus passage, we might say
that honours, or dishonours, are about even. But there is no
comparing the ways in which God responds.

In Exodus 16 God replies with gifts designed to meet the people's
need with beautiful precision, to convince them of his compassion
and his desire and power to save, and to remind them of his glory.
Quails are mentioned at one point, but this story is otherwise
concerned with the gift of manna. Some commentators get so excited
about identifying the stuff with an excretion of insects living on
twigs of the tamarisk, that they do not have time for much else. But
that is a pity, for then they do not see the wood for the trees. The gift
of manna in Exodus 16 is pure miracle. Its timely arrival is not the
only thing to make that clear, of course. When the Israelites go out to
gather it, each of them gathers exactly the right amount for himself
and his family; on the sixth day of the week a double portion is given
and collected so that the sabbath rest can be properly kept; on the
sabbath, appropriately, no manna appears at all; while any kept at
the end of any of the first five days goes bad overnight, the half of the
sixth day's gathering put aside for the sabbath keeps perfectly fresh.
This bountiful God has thought of everything! No wonder they
place some of it in a jar to be kept as one of their holiest objects, a sign
for future generations of the extent of God's grace (no doubt that
manna will remain fresh for ever: yet more miracle!).

Understandably, the extent of the miracle takes some time to
penetrate the minds of some of the Israelite people. Some try to keep
some manna overnight early in the week. Others go in a vain search
for it on the sabbath. They try to manage for themselves something
that cannot be managed, but needs only to be accepted with proper
gratitude and clear insight into the nature of the giver. Their lack of

faith is met with Moses' anger and then with God's exasperation, but nothing more. The offenders are not punished. The futility of their efforts is deemed to be enough to teach them the lessons they need to learn.

In Numbers 11 things are very different. It is almost as if we are dealing with quite another God. In Exodus God's 'hearing' his people's complaints meant salvation and life. Now it means death. First the fire of God's anger burns so fiercely among them, that parts of the camp are destroyed (again we must not try to rationalize these events: they are meant to be seen as miraculous, and whatever we think of such miracle, we must accept the terms in which the story is written). Secondly, at the end of the story he engineers a fall of quails that drives the people mad with greed, and turns quickly to plague in their mouths.

In Exodus the quails were mentioned only in passing. Here the storyteller gives them his full attention. We need to pay heed to the way he writes, for some commentators would lead us far astray. Some of them hardly bat an eyelid, but explain that quails do migrate over the Sinai peninsula, and that they often settle on the ground in large numbers and can be caught very easily. One might go on in that vein to explain that occasional 'wrecks' of birds occur (to use the ornithologists' term), where huge numbers of birds are driven off course by a storm, and end up scattered over the land in an exhausted state. But such rationalizing simply will not do here. According to the story the fallen quails create a pile round the camp many, many miles in diameter, and three feet deep! Never was a wreck seen like that! Other commentators, much more discomfited by these details than their colleagues, have suggested that the storyteller means the birds were *flying* three feet above the ground when they were caught! The New English Bible and its second edition, the Revised English Bible, even introduce 'flying' into their translations. Such silliness, and tampering with the text, will not do either (suffice it to say the word 'flying' nowhere appears in the Hebrew).

The fact is that we have entered here upon the theatre of the absurd, as well as the stage of the miraculous. The fall of birds is meant to be seen as quite ridiculous and wholly supernatural in its proportions. There is a vast humour in the storytelling, though it is of the most grim kind. What is truly disconcerting about the story is the result of the fall, and the divine purpose behind it. A fox in a chicken run, faced with such an unnaturally generous supply of food, will release its instinct to kill until all the birds are dead, and it has far more than it can possibly cope with. The Israelites in Numbers 11 are like foxes in God's chicken run. They collect the quails for two days and a night! They cannot begin to know what they are doing. A sinister impulse to collect and to eat has taken them over. But foxes in chicken runs get shot, and now the Israelites get the plague. What might have seemed a revelation of God's extraordinary generosity has turned out to be another expression of his terrible anger. Our laughter at the fall of birds becomes rotten in our mouths, and dies in our throats. Numbers 11 ends with a fearful seriousness.

The way the storyteller handles Moses' power-sharing in that chapter is consonant with the rest. In the parallel account in Exodus 18, Moses is prompted to act by his father-in-law's concern for his welfare. There is no complaining anywhere, just sensitivity, a proper solicitude, and a suggestion whose good sense is immediately seen, and which is efficiently acted upon. In Numbers the plan of the seventy elders arises as a response to a bitterness in Moses that matches the anger of his God. Driven to despair by the people's weeping he begins to accuse God of laying impossible burdens upon him. 'Am *I* the mother and the nursemaid of all this people?' he asks. Like Cain's terrible question, 'Am *I* my brother's keeper?' Moses' words conceal an accusation, as the emphatic 'I' of the Hebrew again makes clear. Surely it is God, Moses implies, who is their mother and nurse, and as such he, or rather she, must provide food for her people. But Moses does not show much faith in God's willingness to fulfil her duties, and sees death as the only way to find release from his burdens. The wholly negative tone of the passage is only what we might expect from the rest of the chapter. More hopeful, in part, is God's response to Moses. He himself comes up with the plan of delegation, and he empowers the seventy elders for their tasks once they are chosen. Against Moses' expectations he also takes on the task of feeding his people. But at that point hope is cruelly dashed, for the food he supplies is that terrible mound of quails. There is in the end very little to rejoice over in this chapter.

Salvation or destruction: further passages explored

Exodus 16 and Numbers 11 belong to two series of passages which are concerned with God's response to complaints of the people during their years in the wilderness. Of those texts only two, from Exodus 17 and Numbers 20, parallel one another closely in the way that Exodus 16 and Numbers 11 do, but the two series still invite comparison with one another, and that comparison once made produces some highly significant results.

The Exodus series begins on the shore of the Reed Sea. Faced by water in front and Egyptian troops advancing behind, the Israelites panic. 'Is it because there are no graves in Egypt that you have taken us away to die in the wilderness? What have you done to us, in bringing us out of Egypt? Is not this what we said to you in Egypt, "Let us alone and let us serve the Egyptians"? For it would have been better for us to serve the Egyptians than to die in the wilderness.' (Exod. 14.11–12). Again they ignore God's responsibility for their escape, and make their liberation grounds for accusation. Again we see how far the full process of liberation has yet to run. Against their poverty stands the rich faith of Moses. 'Fear not,' he says, 'stand firm, and see the salvation of the Lord, which he will work for you today.' More than any of the other major characters in the great story from Genesis to Kings Moses has a tendency to know what he is talking about. The grim game of salvation is indeed played out before them.

The account of the events at the sea is made up of two versions, quite distinct from one another, but cleverly intertwined. According to one of them God drives back the waters of the sea by a strong east wind, and causes a mysterious panic in the Egyptian camp. Their army flees on to the exposed sea bed, and there gets bogged down. God then makes the wind drop and the waters return, and the entire Egyptian force is drowned. This version says nothing about the Israelites making a crossing. Instead they stand on the shore and watch as their enemies are destroyed. The other version, thanks partly to Hollywood, is the more familiar of the two. Here the waters are split and piled up either side of a pathway across the sea bed. The Israelites take this path and complete the crossing safely, but when the Egyptians pursue them along it, the walls of water collapse and drown them. Again, if we are faithful to the terms of the story, we will refrain from any attempt to provide rational explanations of these events. They are to be regarded as pure miracle, those of the first version as much as those of the second, although it is true that the miracle is heightened in that second account.

After the victory at the sea the triumph song, but hardly have the last notes escaped Israel's lips than we come to the second story of complaint (15.22–7). Three days' journey on into the desert are hurried over in a verse, and then the people run out of water. They find some, but it is not fit to drink. So they 'murmur' against Moses (the same word is used in chapter 16 and Numbers 11) and ask, 'What shall we drink?' Moses appeals to God, who shows him a shrub growing at the spot. He throws it into the water, and that immediately becomes sweet. So the people's thirst is slaked. That is almost all. The tale is told with the utmost economy, as if nothing unusual was taking place. But God goes on to speak to his people of the need for obedience. If it is forthcoming, he will protect them from the terrible plagues with which he afflicted the Egyptians before their escape. '. . . for I am the Lord,' he says, 'your healer.' Thus this demanding people are reminded of the demands made of them, and given more than a hint of how terrible the consequences will be, if those demands are not met. But God does not remonstrate with them. The dominant tone of his speech is not threatening. His business is that of caring, blessing, saving. When they reach their next stopping place, they find not one but twelve springs of fresh water, one for each of their tribes. God is indeed their healer. There can be no doubting it.

But the people do doubt it. Immediately after this story comes that of the giving of the manna, and immediately after that another concerning their complaining about a lack of water (17.1–7). They have moved on from Elim, the oasis of the twelve springs, and have camped at a place called Rephidim. There is no water at all to be seen, but this time, instead of the question, 'What shall we drink?', they issue Moses with an abrupt command: 'Give us water to drink.' Now they do not simply murmur against him, they quarrel noisily with him. Moses does not turn at once to God, their healer, but enters into the quarrel. 'Why do you find fault with me?' he asks, 'Why do you put the Lord to the proof?' His questions reveal to the people the significance of their complaint. It amounts to a lack of faith in a God who has done more than they could have dreamed of to demonstrate his own faithfulness. They are in this wilderness with God, and there is no need to fear. But the people take no notice, and instead turn again to accusation: 'Why did you bring us up out of Egypt, to kill us and our children and our cattle with thirst?' We have heard this before, of course, and so has Moses. At this point he does turn to God, but only to show him that he is at his wits' end, and to express his fear. 'What shall I do with this people? They are almost ready to stone me.' The scene by now is an ugly one. Things here are far worse than in the previous three chapters. Yet still God wears the dress of healer. He tells the despairing Moses to strike a rock with his rod, and water will stream forth from it for the people to drink. Another miracle of salvation occurs.

Numbers 11 begins the second series of wilderness complaint stories. These are more spaced out than the ones in Exodus, and the next one does not appear till chapter 14. By this time they are approaching the borders of the Promised Land, and minds have turned to plans for invasion. Chapter 13 records the sending of spies into the country, to discover how well defended it is. It tells how they returned bearing a huge bunch of grapes, and with reports of a land 'flowing with milk and honey', just as God had promised. But they also brought reports of strong, fortified cities, and inhabitants as big as giants, and these, as chapter 14 now makes clear, make more impact on the people than the assurances of fertility. 'Would that we had died in the land of Egypt!' The old cry, familiar to us from the Exodus stories, now goes up again. 'Or would that we had died in this wilderness! Why does the Lord bring us into this land, to fall by the sword?' (At least they acknowledge God's part in things.) 'Our wives and our little ones will become a prey; would it not be better for us to go back to Egypt? . . . Let us choose a captain, and go back to Egypt.' As on the shore of the Reed Sea, they see themselves facing defeat and extermination in battle. On that occasion Moses urged them not to to be afraid, and God responded immediately by ordering the preparations for his great act of salvation. 'Why do you cry to me? Tell the people of Israel to go forward.' Those were his opening words to Moses then. In Numbers 14 we have a similar pattern. First Joshua and Caleb, two of those sent as spies into Canaan, try to persuade the people to trust in God's protection and to have no fear. After that comes the divine response, but this time not before the people reject Joshua's and Caleb's assurances, and threaten to stone them. When God speaks, his words are devastating. 'How long will this people despise me? And how long will they not believe in me, in spite of all the signs which I have wrought among them? I will strike them with pestilence and disinherit them, and I will make of you' (that is Moses) 'a nation greater and mightier than they.' Thus the promises to Abraham are declared null and void. The great experiment in redemption that began back in Genesis 12 has failed. God has finally lost all patience and all hope.

He began with the man and the woman in the Garden. He began again with Noah. He began a third time with Abraham and the miracle of his son Isaac. Now he means to wipe out his people, as he destroyed his creation in the Flood, and start all over again with Moses. It is a fearful moment in the narrative. But against the poverty of God's hope stands again the faith of Moses. He intercedes on behalf of the people, and he wins some pardon from God. It may, at first sight, not seem a great deal, but in truth it is almost everything. The generation which came out of Egypt will die in the wilderness, but their children, and Joshua and Caleb, will enter the Promised Land. There will after all be no fourth beginning. The ancient promises still stand. God remains commited for good or for ill to his people.

Yet God's pardon does not mean we can put memories of the Flood out of our minds. The people being addressed by this fearful God *will* die in the desert, all of them except only for Joshua and Caleb. For the rest of them the promises have turned out to be empty. They expressed a wish to die in the wilderness; they shall have what they asked for. Twice in the account they hear the terrible words, '. . . your dead bodies shall fall in the wilderness.' They are told that their children will have to endure years of wandering in the wilderness, suffering because of the faithlessness of their parents, until, God tells them, ' . . . the last of your dead bodies lies in the wilderness'. ' . . . You shall bear your iniquity,' he continues, 'forty years, and you shall know my displeasure.' He concludes with a formal oath: 'I, the Lord, have spoken; surely this will I do to all this wicked congregation that are gathered together against me: in this wilderness they shall come to a full end, and there they shall die.' We could not wish for greater clarity.

Moses has managed to change God's mind. God has relented. There is some pardon to be had, and hope for the future. But for the moment there is no act of salvation like that at the Sea. For the moment all the talk, such clear, unambiguous talk, is of suffering and of death. Moses snatches God's plans of redemption from the fire of his anger, but he does not put out the flames. As if to prove that he is in earnest, God immediately afflicts the spies who had caused such panic among the people with the plague. Joshua and Caleb are spared, of course. The rest die on the spot. As if to demonstrate his terrible seriousness, he orders the people to set out the next day ' . . . for the wilderness by the way to the Reed Sea'. From the borders of the Land of Promise they must go back almost to where they came from. They said it would be better to go back to Egypt. They shall very nearly have what they asked for.

But just as the people in Exodus 16, when first given the manna, found it hard to come to terms with God's meticulous generosity, so now they are blinded by the clarity of God's judgement. They only hear half of what God has been saying. They recognize their lack of trust in God's promises. They acknowledge their sin in heeding the warnings and the wild stories of the majority of the spies. But they are deaf to the rest. The promises no longer have any substance for them, but that appalling fact has not penetrated their minds. They turn not to the Reed Sea, but back to plans for invasion. Again like some in Exodus 16 they try to manage things for themselves. The result is inevitable, but this time much more tragic. They enter Canaan without Moses and without their God. They are defeated, and those who can, turn to flight. It is the final twist in the story of this chapter. It could hardly be further removed from the conclusion to the story of the Reed Sea.

Things are bad enough in Numbers 14. If anything they are worse in chapter 16. Near the start of chapter 14 the people spoke of choosing another leader and going back to Egypt. Now rebel leaders appear on the scene and can be named. The chapter is somewhat confusing, for it is a conflation of at least two accounts concerning one rebellion led by Korah the son of Izhar, and another led by Dathan and Abiram. The difficulties and many of the details need not concern us. It will be sufficient for our purposes to point to a few of the features of the chapter as we have it.

It does not begin as a story of the complaining of the people like the others we have looked at so far. It only becomes that towards the end. It starts as a struggle for power, and a challenge to Moses' authority. Korah sets up an alternative people of God (the Hebrew term translated 'company' in the RSV in verse 5 and beyond is the same as 'congregation' in verse 2 and elsewhere, which is used to refer to Israel as a whole). He puts himself forward as its leader. Dathan and Abiram for their part reject Moses' leadership and reproach him with these words: 'Is it a small thing that you have brought us up out of a land flowing with milk and honey, to kill us in the wilderness, that you must also make yourself a prince over us?' It is part of the great skill of the storytellers and the compilers of this material that they repeat events or speeches, but with subtle changes that give the larger narrative not just variety, but tension and further layers of meaning. Dathan's and Abiram's words recall the complaints of the people in three of the Exodus stories and in Numbers 14. But never before has Moses been accused of lording it over the people (some words of Korah in verse 3 of this same chapter come close to such a charge) and never before has *Egypt* been called 'a land flowing with milk and honey'. That description is the one consistently applied by God and Moses to the Promised Land. To apply it to Egypt is to stand the truth on its head, to call bondage freedom, and despair hope. It is to mock the purposes of God.

Shocking though that is, it is not as surprising as God's reaction. He threatens to destroy at one stroke the whole congregation of the people, with the exception only of Moses and his brother Aaron. Their pleading averts such a complete disaster, and succeeds in focusing God's punishment on those who are guilty of the rebellion. Yet that punishment is certainly terrifying enough. As Korah, Dathan and Abiram stand defiantly at the doors of their tents with their wives and children, the ground opens beneath them and swallows them up, together with the tents and all their belongings. The chasm then closes up of its own accord. There is nothing to be seen on the spot but bare earth. It is as if those families had never been. Those who first heard this story would have understood well enough that if the rebel leaders were to be punished, then the other members of their families might have to suffer with them. Their notions of the family as an inseparable unit would have seen to that. But such dramatic descent to Sheol, the land of the dead they believed to be beneath the earth, could not in any way be expected, and in the story it causes panic. Even as the people run away in terror, the fire of God's anger, which destroyed parts of the camp in Numbers 11, now consumes the 250 men who had been the closest supporters of Korah in his bid for power.

Still this appalling tale is not at an end. The next day the people 'murmur' against Moses and Aaron. We are back in the mould of the familiar complaint story. This time their complaint is brief: 'You have killed the people of the Lord.' It is a striking charge. For one thing it overlooks God's clear part in the extraordinary events that they witnessed the previous day. For another it implies their agreement with Korah that he and his followers were indeed the true people of God. Thus it shouts their spiritual blindness, and whispers darkly of their own rebelliousness. But that is again not enough to explain God's reaction. Just as he did earlier in the chapter, he warns Moses and Aaron to 'Get away from the midst of this congregation, that I may consume them in a moment.' Moses and Aaron bravely do not do as they are told, but this time they cannot save the body of the people from disaster. A sudden and miraculous plague breaks out in the camp, and though Aaron, as priest, runs into the midst of the people with ritual of atonement, he cannot stop the pestilence before 14,700 lie dead.

Mercifully, the remaining two complaint stories of the Numbers series are much shorter. The second of them in 21.4–9 recalls in its words of complaint the stories of Exodus 16 and 17 in particular, and also Numbers 11: 'Why have you brought us up out of Egypt to die in the wilderness? For there is no food and no water, and we loathe this worthless food.' It is sometimes said that only the Exodus complaint stories and the one in Numbers 20, which we will come to in a moment, deal with matters of life and death. That is not the case. In Numbers 11 certainly the people do not appear to be faced with starvation. But in chapter 16 Dathan and Abiram make clear that they see only the prospect of eventual death in the wilderness if Moses continues as their leader, and in chapter 14 death in battle seems only too imminent. Here, though it is not true that they have no food, for they still have their daily supplies of the 'worthless' manna, they remain without water, and, manna or no manna, death would seem to stare them in the face. Yet how does God react but by making the desert alive with poisonous snakes! The people's confession and Moses' intercession then result in a God-given means of protection from the effect of the venom. But not before yet again many of the people have died. There is no mention in the story of the giving of water, or of food beyond the manna. The snakes and the tardy remedy make up the entirety of God's response.

The penultimate story of the series (20.2–13) would seem to be the only one to break the pattern. It is a close parallel of the complaint story of Exodus 17. Even the place, Meribah, is the same. (Rephidim came to be renamed Massah and Meribah in the Exodus story). The people are more expansive in their complaining, but their words merely combine elements by now all too familiar. Only their opening wish is new: 'Would that we had died when our brethren died before the Lord!' That is a reference back to the events of chapter 16, and strange though it is, it is no more extraordinary than their wish in Exodus 16 that they had been killed together with the Egyptians at the time of the Passover. At least this time they do not threaten to stone Moses as they did in Exodus 17. It is not the people who break the pattern of the Numbers stories, but God, for he responds almost exactly as he did at Meribah before. We have got so used to untold wrath and destruction, but now God again brings water gushing from the rock, and the people are saved.

But alas, that is not the whole story. Moses is told by God to take his rod and he and Aaron are to address the rock, commanding it to give up its water. We hear of Moses addressing the people instead: 'Hear now, you rebels; shall we bring forth water for you out of this rock?' Then he strikes the rock with his rod, as he did in Exodus, and the water pours forth. Now comes the sting in the story's tail. God speaks to Moses again and to Aaron: 'Because you did not believe in me, to sanctify me in the eyes of the people of Israel, therefore you shall not bring this assembly into the land which I have given them.' It is another devastating speech, and it comes out of the blue. Admittedly Numbers 14 made no mention of Moses and Aaron entering the Land, but talked only of Caleb and Joshua. But nothing has prepared us for this divine outburst. It is indeed not wholly clear from the passage where Moses' and Aaron's fault lies. One can only think it is to do with their not addressing the rock. That is the one thing they are commanded to do together (in the Hebrew the verb of verse 8's 'tell the rock' is in the plural) which the story does not mention their performing. The terms of God's condemnation encourage us also to interpret Moses' address to the people as a cynical expression of a lack of trust in God's power to provide the water, and to suppose that Aaron tacitly shared his disbelief. It is possible, too, that in striking the rock as he was told to do in Exodus 17 Moses this time has further infringed the divine command, though nothing was said explicitly about him not using his rod in that way. When all is said and done, the passage is barely understandable. One suspects that somewhere along the line of the story's forming there has been some attempt to draw a veil over the proceedings, and to protect the reputation particularly of the great Moses. Four other passages in the Old Testament refer to these events, and there are hints in two of them of something more serious than we seem to have here. Numbers 20 itself looks back in verse 24, and talks of Moses and Aaron rebelling against God's command, and 27.14 uses much the same terms. Those do not get us much further. but Psalm 106.33 says, ' . . . for they' (that is the people) 'made his spirit bitter, and he spoke words that were rash' (the verse does not mention Aaron), while most significantly of all Deuteronomy 32.51 speaks of Moses and Aaron 'breaking faith' with God in the midst of the people, and of their 'not revering him as holy'.

Whatever the truth of this particular matter, one thing is plain.

The primary concern of the story in Numbers 20 is not with God's supplying the water, but with Moses' and Aaron's disobedience or lack of faith, and their being barred from entering the Promised Land. The story is not primarily about salvation, but about severe judgement, and it ends in tragedy, in hopes dashed most cruelly to smithereens. The pattern of the Numbers series is dented, but not broken.

Sinai: an attempt at an explanation

The question that now clamours for an answer is clear: why in the Exodus complaint stories does God immediately respond by performing miracles of salvation, while in the Numbers stories he replies with miracles of devastating destruction, or, in the case of Numbers 20, with salvation overshadowed by terrible condemnation? The solution does not lie either with the terms of the complaints made, or with the nature of the people's needs. That, we hope, has become established already. Indeed, we would assert most emphatically that there is nothing within the stories themselves to explain any change in the divine response, let alone a change as complete and as dramatic as the two series report. If there is an answer, then it must lie outside the stories, and in particular in the material that occurs between Exodus 17 and Numbers 11.

Before we turn to that material we must look at the course the narrative has taken since the beginning of Genesis, reminding ourselves yet again of familiar events, and skimming through areas we have not looked at so far.

It moved from hope as high as heaven and a garden bright with love through unutterable sadness, loss, and then violence, to the return to Chaos in the Flood. Noah's family so quickly spoiled the new creation that God then made, and after Babel God began a third time with the calling of Abraham. Several times Abraham brought the purposes of God to the edge of extinction, Isaac's birth introduced yet further tragedy and the keenest disappointment, while how God's promises survived Jacob's cruelty and trickery we shall never know. Between them those three patriarchs displayed all the characteristics which brought God such despair in the earlier stages of the story. Certainly they instituted a new era of divine patience and forgiveness.

With Joseph, however, things took eventually a turn for the better. We have said nothing so far about the Joseph story, and we have no space here to go into any detail. We can only say a little about how that story ended.

It ended with brothers reconciled. Though earlier Joseph's brothers had planned to kill him, and had succeeded in selling him into slavery, the story's final scene in Genesis 50 showed sincere confessions of guilt, moving declarations of love and all fear finally removed. This time reunion and reconciliation were complete. There was none of the disappointment, none of the tragic pretence and exclusion that accompanied the reunion of Jacob and Esau. The brothers' crimes against Joseph were met eventually with a forgiveness as large as Esau's, and this time the forgiveness was received, and given the response it deserved. The bonds linking the brothers ended up stronger than they had ever been. A new honesty, a new understanding, a new maturity of love was created in the family. There was no equivalent to the judgement passed in the Garden, or to that passed on Cain in the field howling with his brother's blood. In Genesis 50, and more tentatively in 45 also, discoveries were made about forgiveness that no-one had seen in Genesis before.

It ended also with reunion between father and son. Jacob was no longer a trickster in the Joseph story, but himself the victim of the duplicity of his sons who convinced him that his favourite Joseph was dead. When at last he came down to Egypt, Joseph showed him all the love and respect that were a father's due, all the love and respect that Ham had failed so conspicuously to show to Noah, and that had been so cruelly denied to Isaac by Jacob himself in his youth. Chapter 48 of Genesis formed a direct counterpart to chapter 27. In both two sons were blessed by a dying father whose sight was failing. In each case the younger son received the greater blessing. Yet in one the father did not know what was going on, and was robbed of all dignity. In the other he remained in full control of events and in full possession of his rightful authority. If the Joseph story told of the healing of conflict among brothers, it told also of the proper fulfilment of the bond between father and son.

Thirdly it seemed to represent the beginnings of the healing of the relationship between God and humanity. Though Isaac turned out not to be God's new Adam, it is possible to say that Joseph did. There was a man at last who could discern the larger purposes of God, and who played his part in them to the full. There was a man who did not insist on managing things for himself. When at the end his brothers poured out their guilt and begged him for forgiveness, he replied with the words, 'Fear not, for am I in the place of God?'

(50.19). We had been waiting all Genesis for words like those. Furthermore, when Joseph explained to his brothers the purposes of God that had been running through the events they had been caught up in, he used terms recalling the promises of Genesis 12: ' . . . you meant evil against me; but God meant it for good, to bring it about that many people should be kept alive, as they are today' (50.20; see, too, 45.4–11). If we ask who the 'many people' were who had been saved from famine through Joseph's foresight and planning, they were not merely Joseph, his father and brothers and their families, but all the people of Egypt. The Joseph story provided by far the most conspicuous example in Genesis of the outworking of the promise to Abraham that through him and his descendants all the families of the earth would find blessing.

Thus the symphony of Genesis ended on a series of strong major chords that sounded high hope for God's purposes and for the redemption of the world. The end of Genesis did not bring us back to the beginning, but it surely left us heading in the right direction.

With the beginning of Exodus all again was spoiled. Hopes were held high for just seven verses. Those ended with the statement, ' . . . the descendants of Israel were fruitful and increased greatly; they multiplied and grew exceedingly strong; so that the land was filled with them.' The promises of God were still on course. But Exodus 1.8 read, 'Now there arose a new king over Egypt, who did not know Joseph,' and then began the story of Egyptian brutality and oppression to which we have already referred, and after that we are back with the tales of the Israelites' stubborn complaining in the wilderness with which we have become so familiar.

Hopes for a time were raised so high. At last, it seemed, the purposes of God discovered a little human co-operation. When those hopes are dashed so soon, not only by a cruel foreign king, but by God's own people, then the story turns to bleak tragedy, and becomes unbearable. Things cannot be allowed to go on as they are. God must teach his people how to fall into step with him, how to requite his love. And so indeed he does.

In Exodus 19, after that first series of complaint stories, the people arrive at Sinai, the Mountain of God, and the rest of the material between there and Numbers 11, including the whole of the book of Leviticus, is concerned with the giving of the torah, God's instructions to his people. He gives them now the fruit of the tree of the knowledge of good and evil. That fruit, impetuously taken in the Garden, brought untold ruin. Here, freely given on God's

Mountain, it spells unimaginable blessings of life lived to the full with God in his Land.

He first teaches his people the boundaries of their relationship with him, in the Ten Commandments. To step beyond those will be to step outside the relationship. Then the features of the ground inside the boundaries are mapped out. The people are taught the implications of the relationship for their worship and their cult, for the ordering of their society, its internal politics and economics and its foreign policy, for their personal relationships with one another, and for their attitudes and inner dispositions. They are shown how the relationship can be kept in good order and repaired by means of a great array of sacrificial rituals, and how the well-being of their society can be maintained. With this great gift of the torah the people are in possession of the secrets of God's heart, and have the means to make of Canaan a new Garden of God.

But this people, though they are led by Moses, are not another Joseph. In the midst of the proceedings, when they have already been given the Ten Commandments and much besides, and Moses is on the summit of Sinai receiving more torah to relay to them, they rebel. The Ten Commandments began: 'I am the Lord your God, who brought you out of the land of Egypt, out of the house of bondage. You shall have no other gods before me' (Exod. 20.2–3). Just twelve chapters later we hear them saying to Aaron, 'Up, make us gods, who shall go before us; as for this Moses, the man who brought us up out of Egypt, we do not know what has become of him.' So Aaron makes a golden calf, and when the people see it, they cry, 'These are your gods, O Israel, who brought you up out of the land of Egypt!'

The story of the golden calf is not quite a complaint story, though it is more terrible than any of them, and as it proceeds shares many of their features, particularly those of the one in Numbers 14. We hear of God's desire to wipe his people off the face of the earth, and begin again with Moses. We hear of Moses' intercession, and his managing, as he will do again, to change God's mind. But when he comes to the foot of the mountain and sees the worship of the calf for himself, we hear the sound of his anger too, and see him smashing the tablets of stone that he has brought down from the summit inscribed with God's torah. Thus he himself acknowledges that the relationship is broken. After that there is widespread slaughter, plague, and God's threatening to send the people on into the Promised Land without him. His tent of meeting, the focus of his presence and means of dialogue, is pitched outside the camp, a sign for all to see of the distance now established between him and his people.

Now at last we can begin to understand the huge discrepancy between the two series of complaint stories and the responses of God they describe. Before Sinai, one could argue, the people had the excuse of not knowing any better. After the giving of God's torah, they know all there is to know. Sinai established, or was designed to establish, the mutual relationship between them and their God, and made clear its demands. To deny the demands of a relationship is to lose the enjoyment of its blessings. Everyone knows that, and the Israelites discovered it for themselves in the wilderness. To deny the reality of the divine love is to enter the dark territory where it cannot be found. They discovered that, too. But they discovered also that beyond God's predictable anger is a surprising mercy.

A God who cannot let his people go

There is more to the story of the golden calf than the features we have already mentioned. When God declares that he cannot accompany his people on their journey into his Land, Moses pleads with him once more, and receives the reply, 'My presence will go with you, and I will give you rest' (Exod. 33.14). When he then asks to see God's glory, it is God's goodness, his graciousness, and his mercy that he sees (33.18–19). Having given Moses a glimpse of that through the fingers of his hand, God commands him to cut two tablets of stone to replace those which were broken. On these are to be inscribed words reminiscent of the Ten Commandments, beginning with a new commandment not to make 'molten gods' (34.1–28). God begins again by not beginning again. He cannot let this people go.

The book of Exodus ends with elaborate details for the construction of a new tent of meeting with all its trappings. There is no mention of it being outside the camp, and instead we are left with the picture of the tent, filled with the glory of God, travelling with the people as they continue onwards (40.34–8).

The book of Leviticus, which follows next, is chiefly concerned with details of how the relationship between God and the people can be repaired and kept in good order. There are elaborate rituals of atonement to be found there. In addition rituals and procedures are laid down for those who have for a variety of reasons become 'unclean', and so have become cut off from the rest of the community. Such rituals and procedures are designed to restore them to their proper place within the people of God and within the inner circle of his blessing. Yet more instructions are given as to how the people should live, how they should avoid oppression, and show true compassion for the poor and the vulnerable. Those instructions include the famous 'Love your neighbour as yourself' (Lev. 19.18). God will not let this people go.

In the midst of those terrifying complaint stories in Numbers is another chapter concerned with the offerings to be made once the people have occupied the Land, offerings which suggest a life of plenty waiting to be enjoyed there (ch. 15). We might say it is galling for people to hear such things when they have been told they will die in the wilderness, but at least the promises of God remain very much in force for their children. That same chapter has more to say about ritual of atonement, and chapter 18 is concerned with the identity and privileges of those who will carry out such ritual, and who will enable the people to dwell with the holiness of God without being destroyed by it. The next chapter is concerned with further provisions for the cleansing and restoration of those who find themselves ritually unclean. Chapter 21 does not deal merely with a desert swarming with snakes, but with another gift of water from God (v. 16), and with a series of military victories which, as we learn at the end, are God's doing more than Israel's (see vv. 21–35 and especially v. 34). Immediately after that comes an extended narrative, containing much wit and satirical humour, about a certain Balak, king of Moab, hiring a seer called Balaam to put the invading Israelites under a divine curse (chs. 22–24). Balak is disappointed. The seer finds the Israelites irrevocably blessed, and the Lord their God in the midst of them. Balaam can do nothing but pronounce God's own words of blessing upon them, while Balak grows ever more frustrated and angry. It is quite clear that God has not let his people go.

The generation that came out of Egypt and took the part of God's bride at the wedding at Sinai (for that is what it was, as the prophet Hosea realized) do indeed die in the desert, as God said they would. But Moses' last act before he dies himself is to teach the torah, Ten Commandments and all, to the new generation born in the wilderness which will cross the Jordan and occupy the Land. That is what the long book of Deuteronomy deals with. It is abundantly clear that this God will never let his people go.

The problem that remains

There is, however, no getting away from it. The memory of fire and plague, of slaughter, gaping earth and venomous snakes, and the great Moses barred from God's land for reasons that are hard to discern and even harder to call sufficient, still haunts our minds, and the stink of those quails will not leave our nostrils. What are we to do with stories like these? We may try to explain them by pointing to the place they occupy in the larger narrative. We may emphasize that they are mingled with and followed by stories of a very different character. But still the question remains: what are we to do with stories like these?

We can, of course, dismiss them from our theology altogether. We can explain that they come from an age when theology and the natural sciences were not divorced from one another, when God was held directly responsible for disasters we would now call 'natural', and for which we would have scientific explanations to hand that did not mention God at all. We could point out further that the ancient Israelites had not yet developed any notion of supernatural evil forces in opposition to God, and that this also encouraged them to see his hand in dark and terrible events.

We can claim that the theology of the Cross forces us now to talk of God in very different ways.

We can, however, if we dare, use these stories in our prayer. Certainly they need very careful handling. Such stories as these of the anger of God have encouraged self-righteousness and vindictiveness, and they still do. They have been cruelly used to put a most unhealthy fear of God into people, or in very recent times in this country to offer absurd explanations for a fire in a cathedral, to denigrate an outspoken bishop, or to hound homosexuals and those suffering from AIDS. Yet we can, and I believe we must, use them in our prayer. To confront the anger of God, not to hurl it in others' faces, but in humility to confront it ourselves, is to find a knife to cut through our pious cant, and a fire to burn up our sentimentality and our complacency. To confront the anger of God in the way the ancient Israelites dared to do, to face it as directed against ourselves and the society of which we are so much a part, is to escape the romantic pretence, the unrelieved jollity, or the easy, unthinking speech of so much that passes for Christian belief and worship. To confront the anger of God is to find some deeper reality about ourselves and our world that we would prefer to forget. It is to

remind ourselves of the radical demands of God, and to realize that
to call the Christian gospel 'good news' is to concentrate on only half
the story. It is to discover something more of the pain of God, the
hurt to which he is so constantly exposed, even now, after Sinai, and
after Golgotha. Above all, and most curiously of all, it is to come to a
deeper knowledge of the inexplicable mercy of God, and of that
fierce love that simply will not let his world go. The writers and
compilers of the stories we have been looking at in this chapter knew
that. That is why, in their work, we will always find God's mercy and
love hiding beyond his anger.

To their extraordinary stories we Christians can add another, of a
man on a cross, whose body is twisted in the shape of God's pain, and
whose eyes blaze with his love and his anger at one and the same
time. To confront *that* figure is so very hard, but it is, I believe, to
confront our salvation, and the salvation of the world.

5

TWO STORIES OF CONQUEST: Jericho destroyed, and God captured

(Joshua 6, 1 Samuel 4)

The crossing of the river

In the last chapter we started off in two relatively small pens, but then escaped and roamed all over the farm. Our discussion this time will restrict itself much more to the two chosen passages, and will need only to take a brief look at a few details of the narratives leading up to them, and at the stories that immediately follow them.

At the end of the book of Deuteronomy Moses climbs up to the summit of Mount Nebo 'which is opposite Jericho' (Deut. 34.1; see also 32.49), and with God's supernatural eyesight is shown by him the whole extent of the Promised Land from Dan in the north to Zoar in the south, and right across to the Mediterranean sea in the west. Now it is time for the new generation born in the wilderness to cross the Jordan, and to begin to take possession of the Land, led not by Moses, of course, since he must die on the wrong side of the river, but by Joshua. We, the readers of the narrative, have been waiting for this moment ever since the concluding words of the book of Numbers: 'These are the commandments and the ordinances which the Lord commanded by Moses to the people of Israel in the plains of Moab by the Jordan at Jericho.' Truth to tell, we have been waiting for it since Genesis 12.

The references to Jericho in both Numbers and Deuteronomy lead us to expect that once the people have crossed the river the city will be the first obstacle in the way of their advance deeper into the

Land. Those expectations are confirmed in the early chapters of Joshua. Before the crossing is made, Joshua sends spies ahead to 'view the land, especially Jericho' (2.2). The rest of that chapter is devoted to the dramatic and somewhat risqué story of their hiding in the house of Rahab, a prostitute in the city, and their escaping by means of a rope let down the walls from one of her windows. Rahab tells them, 'I know that the Lord has given you the land, and that the fear of you has fallen upon us, and that all the inhabitants of the land melt away before you.' In return for her help, the spies strike a bargain with her: she must tie a scarlet cord in the window so that the Israelites can identify her house, and she must gather her whole family together, so that when the city is taken, they can all be spared.

The reports duly brought back to Joshua by the spies are very different from those of their ill-fated counterparts in Numbers 13. Nothing here to strike fear into the hearts of the people. Quite the reverse. So it is that the crossing is made without further ado, 'opposite Jericho' (3.16). The waters of the Jordan are stopped in a heap, and the people cross without getting their feet wet. Thus the miracle at the Reed Sea is repeated. This time, however, there is no panic, no pursuing army. The enemy is on the other side, shut within the walls of Jericho, and the Israelites are ready for war. This is the new generation of the wilderness, the generation which has not known slavery, and which will show no servility. There is no 'murmuring' with them, no wild complaining, no harking back to a mis-remembered past, no rebellion. Instead, quiet obedience (or, as we shall see, noisy obedience when it is required of them), as they and their God go on their way, striking not just fear, but sharp swords into the hearts of the inhabitants of the land.

The taking of Jericho: the origins of the story

When they reach Jericho, five miles the other side of the river, there is no-one to be seen. The inhabitants are hidden behind their city walls, cowering in fear, if Rahab is to be believed.

In one respect here the story is, historically speaking, probably accurate. When the invading Israelite tribes crossed the Jordan and arrived at Jericho, they probably did see no-one there, for the simple reason that Jericho was a deserted ruin. Archaeologists have established that Jericho can claim to be one of the very oldest cities in the world, with a history going back all of ten thousand years. Visitors to the site can climb down a near vertical, uneven stone staircase through the middle of one of the towers of its ancient perimeter wall. I know, because I have done it, and an unforgettable experience it is too. But by the time the Israelites first passed that way, towards, probably, the end of the thirteenth century BCE, that tower, now exposed to view by the archaeologist's shovel, would have been hidden deep beneath the ground, buried beneath layer after layer of the remains of a series of settlements. In the fourteenth century there seems to have been an unfortified village on the site, but by the end of the thirteenth even that had gone. By then it was *at most*, as one commentator has put it, 'the unfortified hangout of a local strongman'.

How then did such a story as that of Joshua 6 originate? We cannot answer that question with certainty, but the details of the story itself would seem to provide us with several clues.

It is striking that it does not mention a battle. There is slaughter well enough, but no battle. The Israelites did have in their possession another account, perhaps two other accounts, of the taking of Jericho which were more conventional. There are hints of one in the story of Rahab and the spies that we have already looked at, hints of an attack mounted on the basis of inside information gathered in that dangerous night of pleasure, or of stealthy entry into the city gained by means of Rahab's treachery. Near the end of the book of Joshua a passing reference is made to a battle, which may or may not belong to the same account as chapter 2: 'And you went over the Jordan and came to Jericho, and the men of Jericho fought against you . . .' (24.11). But in chapter 6 there is no fighting at all, only elaborate processions, the blowing of trumpets, and a great shout. The disorder of battle is missing. Everything is done with calm precision. There are armed men at the front of each procession, and a rearguard, but they do not fight: priests play a far more prominent role in the proceedings. There are seven priests, with seven trumpets, and the whole business takes exactly seven days. On the seventh day they march around the city seven times. The very word seven or seventh occurs twice seven times in the passage.

Throughout the Ancient Near East seven was a sacred number, and it turned up in every area of Israel's worship. Two of the three major annual pilgrim festivals lasted for seven days each, one of them, the Feast of Booths, taking place in the seventh month of the year. The sabbath was, of course, every seventh day. The ceremonies for the ordination of priests or the consecration of altars took seven days. Animals were often offered for sacrifice in sevens, and the blood of sacrifice was on certain occasions sprinkled seven times by the priest.

At the centre of the action in Joshua 6 is the ark, the Israelites' most sacred object of all, the box containing the stone tablets with the Ten Commandments inscribed upon them, the box upon which, so they believed, their God was invisibly enthroned.

The events have, to conclude, all the trappings of a liturgical ceremony rather than a military exercise, and that is almost certainly what lies behind the story, and what gave it its origins.

Between the Jordan and Jericho is the site of Gilgal, at one time a sanctuary of the highest importance in ancient Israel. According to tradition, it was founded by Joshua at the time of the miraculous crossing of the river, and twelve sacred stones were set up there to commemorate the event (Josh. 4.19–24). The people were circumcised there, marked with God's mark as members of his people (5.2–9), and the feast of the Passover was kept there (5.10). Now the Passover was meant to be held annually, and together with the Feast of Unleavened Bread which immediately followed it, was one of the week-long festivals to which we have already referred (see Deut. 16.1–8). When in the early days pilgrims gathered to hold the feast at Gilgal, perhaps their celebrations included a procession round the ruined mound of Jericho, where no walls were any longer to be seen above ground, with the blowing of sacred trumpets of rams' horns, and the solemn carrying of the ark. Psalm 48.12–13 bears witness to a similar procession round the walls of Jerusalem, though in the case of Jericho it would have had the particular significance of a celebration of God's gift of the Land and conquest achieved with his might.

Men and women, young and old, oxen, sheep, and asses

Such, at least, is the likely theory of what lies *behind* the story. But it is not the story itself. For all its curiosities, what Joshua 6 describes, in the form in which we have it, is not a liturgical ceremony, but an act of war, the capture and wholesale destruction of a city. The Jericho of the story is decidedly not deserted. It has its own 'king and mighty men of valour' (6.2; they appear in chapter 2 also). It is well defended, surrounded by high walls, quite beyond the powers of the Israelite tribes to destroy by their own unaided efforts. Though priests play a major role, what is pictured is not high festival, but the deadly business of siege, unusually short, admittedly, and with a remarkable conclusion, but still siege. Whatever our misgivings about the story's historicity (and we make a grave and fundamental error if we think the value of a passage like this is measured by the extent of its historicity), and however confident we might be about its origins, it asks and surely deserves to be taken on the storyteller's own terms.

The first thing to notice about this story of war is its fearful silence about the enemy. The people of Jericho, painted in such bright colours in the story of Rahab and the spies, here feature hardly at all. They are mentioned at the very start, and after that not once until their destruction. That slaughter, when it comes, is reported in the baldest possible terms: ' . . . the people went up into the city, every man straight before him, and they took the city. Then they utterly destroyed all in the city, both men and women, young and old, oxen, sheep, and asses, with the edge of the sword . . . And they burned the city with fire, and all within it.' No heed is paid to their fear, their pain, their grief, their dying. No notice is taken of their humanity. The story pays more attention to the rescue of the single family of Rahab, and to the metallic treasures of the city, than it does to them. After verse 2 even the city itself remains nameless until verse 25, by which time it is all over. Such is the brutality of war, and the anonymity on which it feeds. The storyteller knows what he is talking about.

The second and the most important thing to notice is the part played by God. Before ever the action begins he knows and tells Joshua what the outcome will be: 'See, I have given into your hand Jericho, with its king and mighty men of valour.' He it is who plans what his people will do, and who instructs their general. Joshua fills out the details of the orders, but in doing so clearly reads God's mind, for he comes in for no heavenly rebuke. God, enthroned invisibly upon the ark, is in the midst of it all, and the walls' collapse, engineered so that the Israelites can enter the city from every side at once, is his doing.

Embedded in his initial instructions to Joshua concerning the actions the people are to take on the seventh day we find the clause, ' . . . when they make a long blast with the ram's horn'. The single Hebrew word translated 'when they make a long blast' is a common enough verb meaning to 'draw' or 'drag'. Here it means to drag out the sound, hence 'make a long blast'. It is an imaginative use of the word, but what is significant about it is that it reappears in that sense in only one other place in the Old Testament, in the passage immediately preceding God's appearance on Sinai. There, too, it occurs within divine instructions, not to Joshua, of course, but to his predecessor, Moses: 'When the trumpet' (the Hebrew noun there is in fact 'ram's horn', the same word as is used in Joshua 6.5) 'sounds a long blast, they shall come up to the mountain' (Exod. 19.13). Even the particular part of the verb used is the same in both cases. Such parallels are not accidental. Clearly we are meant by the storyteller to understand the long trumpet blast on the seventh day of the siege of Jericho as heralding an appearance of God to his people rivalling the great theophany of Sinai.

The people's 'shouting with a great shout' or 'raising a great shout' (Josh. 6.5 and 20; the Hebrew uses the same words in each case) confirms this interpretation. We will meet with exactly the same words in the Hebrew again in 1 Samuel 4.5, when the ark is brought into the Israelite camp and, the storyteller reports, 'all Israel gave a mighty shout' (it is a pity that variations in the English translations of the verses obscure the echoes in the original). In each case the shout is far more than simply a war cry. It is a cry of triumph, greeting God's showing himself in the midst of his people.

So the seven-day siege of Jericho ends, as most probably the great festivals of Israel did, with a grand theophany, or an appearance of God. God has been with his people throughout. The ark has been a sign of his presence. But now he appears, or rather the people see the effects of his presence, the sweep of his mighty hand. The walls fall down flat.

The capture of Jericho is clearly God's doing, and the slaughter which follows it belongs to his intentions. This may not be obvious at once. The putting of the city to the ban, or devoting it to the Lord, as the RSV puts it, is part of Joshua's final orders to the people on the seventh day, and receives no mention in God's initial instructions to him. Yet the sequel to the story makes it quite plain that this appalling feast of destruction was in accordance with God's will (ch. 7). After Jericho the next city to be attacked is Ai, but here the Israelite troops are routed, and the people of God have a taste of the fear they have hitherto inspired in others. Joshua's instinct is sure. He knows they have been defeated because they have offended God in some serious way, and become the victims of his anger. In turning to God, and interceding on behalf of the people, as Moses used to do, he discovers the nature of the offence. It is not that they showed no mercy on the streets of Jericho. It is that someone among them has taken for himself some of the treasures of the city which were destined for God's own sanctuary. The culprit, Achan, is duly found, with the treasure buried beneath his tent. Once he and his family and animals are ritually stoned to death and burned and buried under a great heap of stones, then God's anger evaporates, and the people are able to attack Ai again, and deliver up its inhabitants, men, women, and children, to the same fate as met those of Jericho (8.1–29).

God's rules of conquest

In truth we do not need the stories of Achan and Ai to show us the mind of the God of this part of the Genesis—Kings narrative. Deuteronomy has already given us his rules of conquest. In wars against cities outside the Promised Land the people are to enslave the inhabitants, and if they offer resistance, then besiege them and kill all their adult males. The women and children, the cattle and treasures of these cities can be taken as spoil by the people, and kept by them as a gift from their God through whose strength they will have gained the victory. In the case of the cities of the Land, however, the torah, the divine instruction, is more simple: ' . . . you shall save alive nothing that breathes, but you shall utterly destroy them . . . as the Lord your God has commanded' (Deut. 20.16–17; see also Deut. 7:1–2). The reason for such an uncompromising policy is made plain: ' . . . that they may not teach you to do according to all their abominable practices which they have done in the service of their gods, and so to sin against the Lord your God' (20.18; see 7.4).

Such teaching, mercifully, does not accurately reflect what the Israelites achieved, or were able to achieve, in the conquest of the Land. But it remains perfectly understandable, both in terms of the development of the larger narrative, and with regard to the situation of the generation for whom it was first compiled.

After the story of the golden calf, and the tales in Numbers of the people's continued recalcitrance, it is understandable that their God, yearning with such an ancient longing to enjoy requited love, should insist that they be protected *at all costs* from the allurements of other gods, and other religions. A story in Numbers 25 which we did not consider in the last chapter (for it is not a complaint story) makes it even more readily understandable. It tells how the attractions of the women of Moab, a region to the east of the Dead Sea in which the Israelites were encamped, led the people to join in the worship of their gods, and how 'Israel yoked himself to Baal of Peor', the chief of the local deites (25.3). Once again they turned their backs on the God who had brought them out of Egypt, and threw themselves into the arms of another. The God of Deuteronomy, who instructs the new generation before their crossing of the Jordan, knows that the temptations will be far more serious on the other side. He must do all he can to make sure he is not deserted again.

The compilers of the whole narrative, working at the time of the exile in Babylonia, were convinced that the catastrophe had overtaken their people because they and their kings had not been faithful to their God. The ancient teaching given in the wilderness and near the banks of the Jordan had in their minds gone unheeded for centuries. Thus they completed their great work as an act of confession for the sins of the past. But they wrote and edited with their eyes also on the contemporary situation and on the future, with a determination that the people's faith and worship should not be swamped by the religions of their Babylonian masters, and that once back in God's Land, they should not commit the same dreadful mistakes again.

The teaching of Deuteronomy and the theology of the stories of Jericho and Ai and the rest (for the book of Joshua gives us lists of cities put to the ban) are also understandable in terms of ancient conduct of war in that part of the world, or with regard to our own contemporary warfare and religious belief and practice.

In a famous inscription dating from about 830 BCE, known as the Moabite Stone, a king of Moab called Mesha boasts of a campaign against some Israelite towns. Among them was Nebo. 'And Chemosh' (the chief god of Moab, referred to below as Ashtar-Chemosh) 'said to me, "Go, take Nebo against Israel." And I went by night and fought against them from dawn until midday. And I took it and slew them all: seven thousand warriors and old men, together with women and old women and maidens, for I had consecrated it for Ashtar-Chemosh.'

In very recent years holy war has been fought between Iran and Iraq, and with a ruthlessness that has at times, with the use of chemical weapons for example, offended international codes of conduct. In this century, of all centuries, with the unprecedented brutality of its warfare, with its invention of indiscriminate bombing, with its Hiroshima and its Nagasaki, everyone is in a position to understand Deuteronomy and Joshua, and by a most terrible irony the Jews, after the Holocaust, are in one of the best positions of all.

There are also very many Christians who, while not wishing to engage in holy war in the literal sense, are perfectly prepared to crush to powder the cultures of those they convert, and millions more who would condemn those of other faiths as false, if not idolatrous, and who would wish to have nothing to do with them. There are, indeed, Christians of certain sects who would have nothing to do even with other Christians, who do not, for example, allow their children to bring their school friends home, to accept invitations to their parties, or to receive presents from them, even when those friends claim to come from committed Christian homes.

Joshua 6 and the rest are most readily understandable, *and that is precisely why they are so alarming.* Would that we found them totally bewildering! It is their very familiarity which forces us to take them seriously, and to ask whether we can rescue their theology or not.

The fall of the theology of Jericho

That theology has not gone unchallenged, of course. The vigour and profundity of the Old Testament's own challenge is at once realized when we recall how far the ruins of Jericho are from Eden, or from that remarkable declaration of faith in Genesis 1, and how completely the smoke of its destruction hides the last of the promises given to Abraham in Genesis 12. Joshua 6 ends with a curse pronounced over the charred corpses of the city's inhabitants, promising anyone who might rebuild the city that he will do so at the cost of the lives of his own children. Genesis 12 spoke of all the families of the earth finding God's blessing through Abraham and his descendants. We will see in our last chapter that the little book of Jonah, too, has its own challenge to make, and a quite devastating one at that.

Further dissent is found in Jewish writing beyond the Old Testament. In the Talmud, and therefore dating from the very early centuries of the Common Era, there is the following comment on the Exodus story of the crossing of the Sea: ' "When the Egyptian hosts were drowning in the Red Sea," say the rabbis, "the angels in heaven were about to break forth into songs of jubilation. But the Holy One, blessed be He, silenced them with the words, 'My creatures are perishing, and you are ready to sing!' " ' A medieval rabbi makes a similarly significant comment on the Exodus plague stories and a part of the Passover Eve ceremonies. At the Passover Eve meal the stories of the plagues are recited, and with each one a finger is dipped in a glass of wine and a drop of the wine let fall on to a plate. The rabbi explains the custom by saying that Israel's cup of joy cannot be full if her triumph involves suffering, even for her enemies.

The New Testament, despite its talk of God condemning the wicked to an eternity of weeping and gnashing of teeth in the fires of hell (a level of violence, as one commentator has put it, surpassing anything spoken of in the Old Testament), has yet more challenges to offer, and not just in the Passion narratives. In our third chapter we described Esau as 'a bystander on the edge of God's purposes', one who 'suffered grievously that those purposes might go forward'. The Gospels present us with a picture of Jesus of Nazareth searching out those left on the edge, and bringing them into the heart of God's kingdom. They record him burning with anger against those who practised their faith at the expense of others. In these respects this Jesus strikes at the heart of the Jacob/Esau stories, and must present the most radical challenge to the story of the people of Jericho, who are not even left as bystanders, but are trampled into God's ground and burnt to a cinder.

Yet is it not at the foot of the Cross that the theology of Joshua 6 falls and dies? Does not the Cross reveal a God who is victor, to be sure, but only by means of himself becoming the victim of brutality? If in the end we wish to locate God in the destruction of Jericho, should we not search for him lying in the dust with the rest of his people of that city, like them hacked to pieces?

Threat from the Philistines and from corrupt priests

In these brief forays of ours into the territory of Old Testament storytelling we do not, in fact, have to wait until Jonah to find the theology of Joshua 6 again under question. 1 Samuel 4 does not present a direct challenge to the earlier passage. Yet as another story of war, and of God's involvement in war, it has a very different tale to tell.

Joshua 6 belonged to the very beginning of the story of conquest and settlement. 1 Samuel 4 comes well on into it. Entry into the Land lies long in the past, and the task has become one of establishing a secure hold upon it. The enemy threatening that task is at this point the Philistines. We first hear of clashes between the Israelites and the Philistines in the book of Judges, and in particular in the Samson stories (chs. 13–16). In these colourful tales, which we might almost believe were collected from early copies of ancient Israelite boys' comics, Samson wages a one-man war against the Philistines, who are represented as having control of the country. 1 Samuel 4 renews the story of the conflict between the two peoples, and that rivalry remains a major feature of the account of Saul's reign, and does not come to an end till victories won by David, described in 2 Samuel 5.

The Philistines, who via the Greek came to give their name to the land of Palestine, settled in the southern part of the coastal plain from, in contemporary terms, the Gaza Strip to Tel Aviv. They spread there from the area of the Aegean at about the same time as the Israelite tribes themselves moved into the land from the east.

The first three chapters of 1 Samuel are mainly concerned with the birth of Samuel, his boyhood and his call. Samuel does not feature at all in the story with which we are concerned, nor in its immediate sequels. But there are a few details of chapters 1–3 which we should mention.

The action described in them takes place at the sanctuary of Shiloh, where the priest is an old man called Eli. He is assisted in his priestly functions by his sons, Hophni and Phinehas. In chapter 2 those two men are roundly condemned as 'worthless', as putting their own profit before the service of God, and as having sexual relations with some women serving the sanctuary. Eli himself for the most part does not appear in a bad light, but as the one responsible for the proper functioning of the sanctuary, he is implicated in his sons' guilt, is at one point accused of sharing their greed, and is doomed to share in great disgrace about to befall his family. In the last part of the chapter it is prophesied that Hophni and Phinehas will both die by the sword on the same day, and that Samuel will be put in Eli's place as God's priest.

Chapter 3 gives us one more piece of information about Shiloh: the sacred ark is being kept there (v. 3). That will turn out to be of huge significance for the action of chapter 4. In its famous account of the call of Samuel, it also repeats the judgement upon Eli and his sons. This time it comes from God's own lips, the crime of Hophni and Phinehas is declared to be blasphemy, Eli is condemned for not restraining them, and the speech ends with a divine oath making it irrevocably clear that there is nothing these three priests can do to ward off the coming disaster. There is a discomforting hint of what the scale of that disaster will be. The opening words of God's speech

TWO STORIES OF CONQUEST 99

to Samuel are these: 'Behold, I am about to do a thing in Israel, at which the two ears of every one that hears it will tingle' (v. 11). The tremors to be caused by the fall of the house of Eli will shake the whole people.

Thus the storyteller and the compiler create in us, step by fearful step, a sense of foreboding, and when we learn at the start of chapter 4 that the Israelites are going into battle with the mighty Philistines, then our knees begin to tremble and we dread what the outcome might be.

Yet there is one passage in chapters 1–3 which might seem to dispel all fear, and might lead us to expect Israel to win a resounding victory. Chapter 2 begins with a psalm (vv. 1–10). (There are several psalms in the Old Testament outside the Book of Psalms. We will meet another, a wonderfully mischievous example, in Jonah.) It is known as 'The Song of Hannah', for it purports to be a psalm of thanksgiving sung by Samuel's mother after the birth of her long-prayed-for son, and his dedication to the service of God at the sanctuary of Shiloh. It is chiefly famous among Christians as the clear basis for the text of the Magnificat. Though put beautifully into the mouth of Hannah by the storyteller, it did not have its origins with her, but, to judge from its mention of the king at the end, must have been composed for national celebration at some point during the time of the monarchy. It rejoices in the unrivalled might of Israel's God, the creator of the world, and in his habit of turning human affairs upside down and bringing the powerless to positions of strength.

My mouth derides my enemies,

says the speaker (originally, perhaps, the king) at the beginning,

because I rejoice in thy salvation . . .

The bows of the mighty are broken,
but the feeble gird on strength . . .

He will guard the feet of his faithful ones;
but the wicked shall be cut off in darkness;
for not by might shall a man prevail.
The adversaries of the Lord shall be broken to pieces;
against them he will thunder in heaven.

Strong encouragement indeed for little Israel, so often in her history the football in matches played by powers far greater than her. Put in the context of 1 Samuel 1–3, however, and the preparations for battle in chapter 4, its message is more uncertain. On the one hand it would seem clear that the Philistines will have no earthly chance against Israel and this mighty God of hers. These lords of God's Land, as they are portrayed in Judges, will be brought low, and poor, feeble Israel will be exalted. Yet we hear so much in chapters 1–3 of the faithlessness of men in high positions in Israel (chapter 4 will tell us that Eli was not only high priest at Shiloh but for forty years 'judge' in Israel, the one in whom resided the greatest political and spiritual as well as judicial authority among all the tribes). 'He will guard the feet of his faithful ones; but the wicked shall be cut off in darkness,' says the psalm. Given what we have heard about Eli and his sons, and in the light, also, of those dark prophecies of doom, what message do those words convey as Israel goes into battle with Philistia? Do they augur victory or defeat for the Israelites? Those are the questions the storyteller and compiler leave in our minds as we enter the action of chapter 4.

God's capture

They seem to be answered almost at once. Battle is joined, and Israel is defeated with considerable loss of men.

But this, of course, is only the beginning of the story. The Israelite survivors of the battle return to the camp and report the dreadful news. The reaction of the elders is very interesting. 'Why,' they say, 'has the Lord put us to rout today before the Philistines? Let us bring the ark of the covenant of the Lord here from Shiloh, that he may come among us and save us from the power of our enemies.' Had the Israelites been polytheists, like all the other peoples of the ancient world, a natural conclusion to have drawn from the defeat would have been that their god or gods had been overcome by the gods of the Philistines. Their monotheism made such a notion impossible, and instead they had to blame either themselves, or God, or both. Today we might suggest that the reason lay with them. At this period the Philistines were better armed than the Israelites (see 1 Sam. 13.19–22), and their soldiers were more experienced and better organized. But the elders of 1 Samuel 4 put the blame on God. 'The Lord' has put them to rout. Yet it does not occur to them that God might have brought about the defeat as an act of judgement upon them, and unlike Joshua and the elders in the story of Ai in Joshua 7, they do not bother to turn to God to discover his mind. Instead they send to Shiloh for the ark.

Their theology is simplistic and confused. Despite suggesting that God must have been on the side of the Philistines in the battle, they talk as if God is literally enthroned above the ark, and the bringing of it to the camp will mean the bringing of God himself. They seem to think that all they need to do is fetch God and all will be well. Maybe they simply see the ark as a visible guarantee of God's presence and of victory, but that understanding of it is no better, for then they turn it into an idol, ascribe to it magical powers, and leave us asking why they did not take it into battle in the first place. Whatever their reasoning, they seek to make sure that God is on their side. They seek to use God's power to establish their own. Their views are readily recognizable in a world where the fuss about the Turin Shroud has reminded us of a time when high hopes and claims of miracle were commonly attached to pieces of the true cross or heads of John the Baptist, where much Christian literature promises believers great success in life if only they have enough faith in God, and where men and women of political power still try to have God and his Church on their side, and to use their authority to enhance their own. Some readers of 1 Samuel 4 might dismiss the elders as 'primitive'. They are, in fact, perfectly contemporary.

At first the storyteller, with considerable mischief, plays along with them. He hurries over the journeying to and fro. Shiloh was some twenty miles from the camp, but the storyteller does not dwell on the sight of the Israelites (and the Philistines, too!) twiddling their thumbs while the runner and then the ark are on their way. When the ark arrives, however, he slows the pace right down. He gives it its full title: 'the ark of the covenant of the Lord of hosts, who is enthroned on the cherubim'. What fine, solemn words these are! How well they remind us of the purpose for which the ark has been fetched! No wonder its coming puts the fear of God into the Philistines! The Israelite army greets it with the same great shout as bounced off the walls of Jericho and heralded their demolition. The Philistines' camp is close enough for them to hear the noise, and when they learn its meaning they are afraid and say, 'A god has come into the camp.' They are polytheists, of course, and to them the ark means only 'a god'. Yet they have heard of this particular god, and what they have heard only increases their fear. According to Rahab, the Jericho prostitute, the people of her city had had news of the way the Israelites had come out of Egypt, and their hearts had melted and their courage had evaporated away (Josh. 2.9–11). So with the Philistines. 'Woe to us!' they say, 'For nothing like this has happened before. Woe to us! Who can deliver us from the power of these mighty gods?' (Even worse: it is not just a god now, but gods!) 'These are the gods who smote the Egyptians with every sort of plague in the wilderness.' They have not quite got their history sorted out, but they are near enough. Plagues in the wilderness will do. All they can think of is getting the adrenalin going with some warlike talk. 'Take courage,' they say to one another, 'fight,' and 'be men.' Twice they use those words 'be men', and the repetition only serves to underline their predicament. Men they are, and men is all they can be, yet, on their own admission, they must fight against 'mighty gods'.

Battle is joined again, and surely after this we know what the result will be. The storyteller has included only one hint that things might turn out otherwise. When the ark is sent for, he remarks that it is accompanied on its journey to the Israelite camp by Hophni and Phinehas. But he does not remind us of the prophecy that hangs over them, or of the judgement pronounced by God upon the house of Eli. Quickly he immerses us in the euphoria of the Israelites and the terror and bravado of their enemies. Battle is joined again, and surely we know what the result will be.

But the storyteller has been using all his art to lead us up the garden path. With the utmost economy, of the kind we have already seen used to such effect in other Hebrew narratives, he reports the battle. 'So the Philistines fought, and Israel was defeated, and they fled, every man to his home; and there was a very great slaughter, for there fell of Israel thirty thousand foot soldiers. And the ark of God was captured; and the two sons of Eli, Hophni and Phinehas, were slain.' Thus the prophecy of chapter 2 and the dark words of God of chapter 3 find fulfilment, our expectations are overturned, and the elders of Israel are taught that their God is beyond their manipulation.

Much later in the books of Samuel we find another story concerning the ark which reminds us of the battle with the Philistines. It occurs in the account of the chaotic part of David's reign when his own son Absalom is fighting to usurp the throne. At the lowest point in David's fortunes he is forced to evacuate Jerusalem. As he reviews the sad procession of his supporters leaving the city, he finds at the rear two priests and the Levites bringing out the ark. He tells them to turn back, and return the ark to its place in the temple. 'If I find favour in the eyes of the Lord, he will bring me back and let me see both it and his habitation; but if he says, "I have no pleasure in you," behold, here I am, let him do to me what seems good to him' (2 Sam. 15.25–6). The David of 2 Samuel is far from being an exemplary character, yet here in the gloom of the surrounding narrative we have a bright flash of faith, wisdom and humility. David has mastered the lesson which the elders of 1 Samuel 4 needed to learn. He refuses the attempt to turn God into his puppet.

Death, birth, and death again

The rest of 1 Samuel 4 is devoted to underlining the apparent enormity of the disaster it has described. It does it by telling two stories about the reception of the news of the battle. The first concerns Eli. Though he sits by the gate of Shiloh, in his blindness watching the road, he is nearly the last in the town to hear the news. Some commentators have wondered aloud why this should have been so. Did the runner bringing the news from the battlefield run straight past him when he reached the town? Was silly old Eli sitting at the wrong gate? We can safely dismiss these questions. Eli is left nearly to the end in the storyteller's cause of dramatic tension and suspense. It does not matter why the news reaches him so late. It matters only that it does.

The first he knows that something is up is when he hears a great cry of anguish from the town. The runner has gone into it and told the story of the battle. Like the Philistines when they heard the shout greeting the ark's arrival in the Israelite camp, Eli asks, 'What is this uproar?' Like the Philistines he is filled with terror. The storyteller has already told us that he has been watching the road, his heart trembling with fear for the precious ark. Unlike those of the Philistines his worst fears have been realized, and the cry he hears go up in the town is not for the ark's arrival, but for its capture.

Dead on cue the runner hurries over to Eli to answer his question. Again the story demands the coincidence that he is on hand, and can catch the question above the uproar. Again such implausible details do not matter. They help to make the story, they do not mar it. To increase the suspense the storyteller again slows the pace. He tells us first of Eli's great age and of his blindness. Then the runner introduces himself. Then Eli asks how the battle has gone. Then, and only then is the devastating news given to the old man. Quite deliberately the storyteller has not reported what the runner told the people of the town. We have learned only that he 'told the news', and that the people cried out in anguish. To have given full details at that earlier point would have been to remove the sting from the report to Eli, and spoil its shock.

The words of the runner to Eli are very close to those the storyteller used himself a few verses before to describe the outcome of the battle. But there are subtle differences, and one of particular significance. 'Israel has fled before the Philistines, and there has also been a great slaughter among the people; your two sons also, Hophni and Phinehas, are dead, and the ark of God has been captured.' No mention now of the numbers of troops or military units slaughtered (the Hebrew term translated 'thousand' in verse 10 might well mean military unit in that context). That, to the high priest of the sanctuary of Shiloh, is not the most important item of news. There is mention of Hophni and Phinehas, of course. But now they do not come at the end of the list. There is a fearful crescendo in the messenger's speech, such as we noted in the command of God to Abraham in Genesis 22.2. The worst news of all is left till last. Eli has been trembling with fear for the ark. No word has been said about his fears for his sons. It is as if he gave them up for dead when they left Shiloh. All his fear is concentrated on the ark which he, being too old and frail to accompany, delivered to their charge. If he now grieves for them, we do not hear of it. Indeed there seems no time for such grief, for at the news of the ark he collapses, falls backwards from his seat, breaks his neck, and dies. So a further part of the prophecy of chapter 2 and the divine judgement of chapter 3 comes to its dark fruition.

But still the house of Eli has not seen the last of it. The news of the capture of the ark, and of the deaths of Eli and Phinehas, is taken to Phinehas' wife, nine months pregnant with his second son. Not surprisingly the shock brings on premature labour. She is safely delivered of a son, but despite the encouragement of the midwives she takes no notice of the baby. There is no joy at this birth, no laughter, only grief, the naming of the child, and then the death of the mother. The woman is not given a name herself. The story is not interested in her for herself. But nor is it interested in her son, only in the timing of his birth and his name. With almost her last breath she calls him Ichabod, saying, 'The glory has departed from Israel!' The storyteller explains her words by referring to the deaths of her

father-in-law and husband, as well as the capture of the ark. But in
the last sentence of the story he has her say, 'The glory has departed
from Israel, for the ark of God has been captured.' No mention of Eli
and Phinehas now. Clearly it is the fate of the ark that has provoked
the name Ichabod, and that has led to her death, just as it killed her
father-in-law.

'The glory has departed from Israel' is meant to be an explanation
of the name Ichabod, which means either 'No Glory', 'Where is the
Glory?', or 'Alas for the Glory!'. The word 'departed', used in the
RSV and other versions, does not quite convey the sense of the
Hebrew verb, which means 'gone into exile'. There is a hint in the
Hebrew of a future homecoming not given by the more final-
sounding 'departed'. Yet it is the merest hint of hope in a story of
otherwise unbroken tragedy. It is but the momentary flicker of a
candle in the dark.

'Are we still the people of God?'

Why does the capture of the ark cause quite so much consternation?
That might seem a needless question to ask. We understand how
deeply people can become attached to sacred objects. We can
imagine the horror that would ripple through Christendom if the
Turin Shroud were stolen, even though its direct connection with
Jesus has been disproved by the scientists. We know that a nation's
sense of its own identity can become bound up with material objects,
the identity of the British with the Crown Jewels, that of the Greeks
with the Elgin Marbles, that of the people of Hungary with the
Crown of Stephen. Yet the significance for the ancient Israelites of
the capture of the ark went beyond the scope of such attachments. It
posed for them the question, 'Are we still the people of God?'

1 Samuel 4 began with the Israelites being defeated in battle and
with their elders talking of God fighting on the enemy side. When it
reported the result of the second engagement, it used a word which
the Philistines in their terror had applied to what God had done to
the Egyptians. Unfortunately the RSV is forced by the sense of the
narrative to obscure the play on words by translating the term as
'plague' the first time round (v. 8), and 'slaughter' the second (v. 10).
'These are the gods,' say the Philistines, 'who smote the Egyptians
with every sort of plague (*maccah*) in the wilderness.' 'So the
Philistines fought,' says the narrator, 'and Israel was defeated . . .
and there was a very great slaughter (*maccah*).' The Hebrew

conveys, as the English cannot, the notion of tables being turned, of the people of God becoming now the enemy of God. Israel has, in God's eyes, so it seems, become another Egypt, deserving of a similar fate. Such, at least, is the suggestion of that play on words. Put it together with the talk after the first battle, and add to it the understanding of the ark as the throne of God, as the visible guarantee of God's presence with his people, the symbol of his covenant relationship with them, as their wedding ring, we might say, and you have then something to explain the consternation of Eli and the wife of Phinehas.

Can Israel still be the people of God, or has God chosen the Philistines instead? That is the question this chapter leaves us, and it is the question that it left those who first heard the larger narrative being read. For them it was a particularly poignant one. They, or their parents or grandparents, had seen Jerusalem captured, its temple destroyed, and the ark of the covenant taken into exile by the enemy. They had heard, or heard of, prophets such as Jeremiah or Ezekiel speaking of God being behind the disaster, of him fighting on the enemy side. 'Are we still the people of God?' was for them very far from being an academic question, but was in urgent need of an answer.

A God too hot to handle

It finds an answer in many places in the larger narrative, and one of those places is in the dark comedy of the two chapters immediately following our chosen passage.

If the God of 1 Samuel 4 refuses to play Israel's game, in chapter 5 he refuses to play Philistia's. The ark turns out to be decidedly too hot to handle. The Philistines carry it from their camp to the town of Ashdod, and there they put it in the temple of their god Dagon. That is only what we would have expected them to do. When one people defeated another in the Ancient Near East it was usual for the victors to place in their own temples the sacred figures of the gods of the vanquished. It meant that those figures were properly housed, but it was also a clear sign that the defeated gods were henceforth under the authority of their own gods, and the defeated people under their thumb. The Philistines in the narrative of 1 Samuel have no image of the Israelites' god, Yahweh, but they understand, or think they understand, the significance of the ark, and regard it as a convenient substitute.

In truth they do not begin to realize what they are dealing with, but they soon find out. The morning after the ark is put in Dagon's temple, they discover the figure of their great god sprawled on the floor, his face to the ground, in what would have been readily seen as an attitude of worship. They put Dagon upright again, but the next morning they find him in an even sorrier state. Not only has he again fallen flat on the ground, but his head and his hands have broken off and lie at the entrance of the building. Two days before Dagon seemed Yahweh's conqueror. Then he became Yahweh's worshipper. Now he is Yahweh's sacrificial victim.

That will not do, and when, to make matters considerably worse, bubonic plague breaks out in the town, the people of Ashdod decide to get rid of the ark. So it goes south to Gath, but it takes the plague with it, together with an unearthly confusion and terror. It goes north again, to the town of Ekron, but the same things happen there. 'Send away the ark of the God of Israel,' the people cry, 'and let it return to its own place, that it may not slay us and our people' (5.11). An understandable reaction, and it is understandable, too, that none of the other towns of Philistia bid to house the ark instead. Thus it turns out that chapter 6 is concerned with the elaborate preparations for the ark's return, and with its re-entry into Israelite territory.

Before the ark disappears from the narrative for the time being (it does not play a major role again until its triumphal entry into Jerusalem in 2 Samuel 6, though it does feature in another battle with the Philistines in 1 Samuel 14), it leaves behind one more reminder that it is not to be trifled with. The first place it reaches in Israelite territory is Bethshemesh. There some of the inhabitants commit some kind of sacrilege which it is hard for us now to decipher. (The RSV seems clear enough when it speaks of them looking into the ark (6.19), but the Hebrew will not really bear that sense, and would suggest they merely looked at it. But that is not sufficient to explain the subsequent outburst of divine anger.) Whatever the nature of the crime, its consequences are all too plain. Seventy people die on the spot, and the town, far from celebrating the ark's return, finds itself in mourning. Exactly like the Philistines of Ashdod, Gath and Ekron, its people decide to get rid of the ark as quickly as they can. So men come from nearby Kiriath-jearim to collect it, and there at last, without accompanying plague, confusion, or slaughter, it comes to rest.

To those who first heard the narrative in its finished form the significance of these last few stories must have been abundantly plain. If 1 Samuel 4 left them asking whether they could still regard themselves as the people of God, chapters 5 and 6 reassured them that their God had certainly not gone over to the Babylonians. Indeed, their conquerors would soon find him too much to handle, and his term of exile and the exile of his people would eventually come to an end.

Yet the last in the little series of stories about the ark would have recalled to their minds the story of chapter 4, and would have reminded them that though they were irrevocably, for better for worse, for richer for poorer, the people of God, they did not have God in their pocket, and could never keep him there.

If Joshua 6 represents God as mixed up in humanity's games of power and violence in a way that is denied by the Crucified God of the Gospels, 1 Samuel 4–6, in both its tragedy and its comedy, would declare his refusal to play along with us on our terms, and his insistence on doing his own thing. Whether we would today happily regard bubonic plague, panic, and slaughter as examples of his doing his own thing is another matter, of course. But even if we do not, we must surely take seriously the witness those chapters bear to the freedom of God, particularly since we are still so prone in our self-important humanity to attempt to manipulate him.

6

GOD'S FOOL and lessons from an enemy

(1 Kings 19: 1–18, 2 Kings 5)

Getting through to God

'Outside Eden meeting God is problematic. Men and women will have to live in hope that God will search them out. No longer is there an inevitability about the encounter.' That is what we wrote towards the end of chapter 1 as part of our comment on the man's and woman's expulsion from the Garden. And yet in chapters 2 and 3 we saw pictured in the Abraham and Jacob narratives relations of astounding intimacy between God and human beings. God speaks with Abraham and Sarah, he appears to them, he even, admittedly in disguise, sits and eats the meal they set before him. Later, at the Jabbok, Jacob has him in a wrestling hold. When, after Genesis, the story becomes an account not of a family but a people, we are still told of Moses disappearing into the cloud of God's presence on the summit of Sinai. 'Thus the Lord used to speak to Moses face to face, as a man speaks to his friend', says the storyteller (Exod. 33.11). God tells him all the secrets of his heart, and he comes down from the mountain with the skin of his face shining with his glory (Exod. 34.29–35). Yet with this Moses an era has ended, and another finishes with his death.

In Genesis, both before the expulsion from the Garden and after it, relations between God and human beings have an immediacy, a directness, a naturalness about them which beyond Genesis only Moses enjoys. In Genesis there are no priests except in cultures already long-established, those of pre-Israelite Jerusalem where Melchizedek is priest-king (Gen. 14.18), or Egypt (41.45; 46.20; 47.22; etc.). Only once does the word 'prophet' occur, and when it does it jars upon the ear, for it seems curiously out of place, and not to belong to the world of Genesis at all. In a dream God appears to Abimelech and tells him that the woman he has taken into his harem is not Abraham's sister but his wife. 'Now then,' he tells him, 'restore the man's wife; for he' (that is Abraham) 'is a prophet, and he will pray for you, and you shall live' (20.7). The words sound decidedly odd in a story of direct encounter between Abimelech and God, and in a world which had no need of intermediaries to keep open the lines of communication between heaven and earth.

At Sinai, however, the role of intermediary is precisely the one that Moses plays. He it is, and he alone, who runs back and forth between God and the people. At one point his brother Aaron, a certain Nadab and Abihu, and seventy of the elders of Israel are permitted to climb Sinai, there to see God, to catch something of his glory, and to feast in his presense (Exod. 24.9–11). But this is a unique moment of privilege, whose effect on the hearer or reader of the narrative is at once reduced by the compiler following it with material having the more usual description of Moses going up into the heart of the divine presence on his own (24.12–18). As for the mass of the people, they must wait at the foot of the mountain, forbidden even to touch its rock so charged with the holiness of God, at times overawed, even terrified by the trappings of God's appearing (Exod. 19.16; 20.18–20), at others, such as that of the making of the Golden Calf, strangely and shockingly heedless of it all.

After Moses' death, though God accompanies his people, and wields his might or his mischief in the midst of their battles, never again do we come across an individual who enjoys quite such intimacy with him. The business of mediating between him and the people itself becomes institutionalized. The very torah received on Sinai has a great deal about priests, their duties, their rituals, and all their sacred paraphernalia, and once the story gets near the founding of monarchy in Israel, then professional prophets begin to appear on the scene. We find them living together in groups attached to sanctuaries, and then we find them at court, paid by kings and queens to discover the mind of heaven, and to attempt what those elders attempted in battle with the Philistines, to gain access to divine power and use it to support royal or national ambitions.

Yet there remain in the story some whose relations with God have a freshness and a simplicity that remind us of Moses, and behind him of Jacob and Abraham, of Noah and the man and the woman in the Garden. Gideon, the hero of early wars against the Midianites, is one (Judges 6–8), Samuel is another, and undoubtedly Elijah and Elisha, the central characters in the stories chosen for this chapter, are two more.

The history behind Elijah's story

Elijah appears on the scene without any proper introduction as soon as the notorious Ahab is on the throne of Israel and married to the even more notorious Jezebel.

Israel in this context no longer means the entire people of God. They were united under one monarch for a remarkably short time. Amidst seamy court intrigue David was succeeded by his son Solomon, and of him the story presents two distinct pictures (1 Kings 3–11). As far as later tradition was concerned, the more influential of the two was that of a king of exceptional wisdom, learning, wealth and power, a king who understood the meaning of humility and acknowledged his utter dependence on God. The Solomon who had the most influence on political developments, however, was the Solomon of the other picture, the absolute ruler who used forced labour to build his palace and the temple in Jerusalem, who surrounded himself with all the trappings of power, including a vast harem, and who poured the resources of his kingdom into establishing and maintaining large military forces on land and sea. In 1 Kings this picture is muted, its colours obscured somewhat by those of the other. But the consequences of Solomon's reign are writ plain for all to read: civil war and the break-up of the kingdom into two, Israel in the north, and Judah in the south (1 Kings 11–12). Solomon had ridden rough-shod over the old tribal loyalties, and broken the backs of the people under the weight of taxation, forced labour, and military service.

Ahab reigned for twenty years in the northern kingdom in the second quarter of the ninth century BCE. Judged by the criteria of modern western historians he and his father, Omri, were among the greatest kings the Israel of the north ever had.

Omri came to power on the back of anarchy and civil war, and yet in a short reign of only eight years succeeded in uniting the kingdom and in extending and securing its boundaries. He built a fine new capital on the hill of Samaria, and was responsible for great public works in other cities. He formed new trade links with the Phoenicians on the Mediterranean coast, so that a merchant class arose in Israel and introduced a level of prosperity not seen before.

For over a century after his death, long after his dynasty had disappeared, the Assyrians referred to Samaria in their records as 'the House of Omri,' and to the kingdom of Israel as 'the land of Omri.'

When Ahab came to the throne, he carried on where his father left off. He ensured that Samaria was left with fortifications of immense strength, and with palace buildings whose walls and furniture were decorated with inlaid ivory carvings of considerable sophistication and beauty. He enlarged other cities and made them strong enough to withstand the new siege weapons being developed in that part of the world, and significantly increased his kingdom's military resources. Near the southern border of his territory he rebuilt Jericho, which had remained a ruin since the time of Joshua. Though, because of the aggression of the Syrians, he could not give his people lasting peace, he developed further links with the Phoenicians by marrying Jezebel, the daughter of the king of Tyre, much to the benefit of Israel's new merchants. 'The difficult foreign and internal political problems which confronted the northern kingdom . . . required a high degree of political ability and wisdom of the kings from the house of Omri. The Omrides were not found wanting in those qualities, least of all Omri himself and his son Ahab. They belong to the most gifted and energetic rulers who ever occupied Israel's throne.' That comment from Herbert Donner, a Professor of Old Testament at Tübingen University in West Germany is echoed by many other historians.

It is not echoed by the writers and compilers of the books of Kings. 1 Kings 16 describes Omri's rise to power, and then devotes precisely six verses to his reign, mentioning none of his achievements except for the founding of Samaria, and giving that no praise. He is summarily dismissed as leading Israel into idolatry. And if Omri is judged by silence, Ahab is condemned by the loud abuse of six chapters claiming that his polices struck at the very heart of the nation's life, and precipitated the most serious crisis in the history of the people of God since the making of the Golden Calf at Sinai.

Jews and Arabs live together, often all too uneasily, in Israel today. In the ninth century BCE Omri and Ahab were faced with the problem of uniting and then holding together territory still occupied by both Israelites and Canaanites. A line of Canaanite cities ran right through the centre of the kingdom, with their distinctive culture, and without the worship of the Israelite God, Yahweh. The business of conquest as outlined in Deuteronomy and Joshua was still, in fact, far from complete. It seems that Omri and Ahab attempted to gain the support of both groups of the population by retaining Jezreel as the capital of the Israelite part, and by founding Samaria as a new Canaanite city-state, and capital for the Canaanite communities. Among the Israelites the kings behaved like Israelites, or tried to, but in their Samaria Ahab built not a temple to Yahweh, but one to Baal, probably here to be identified with the chief god of Tyre, Melqart. It was natural, only courteous, that he should provide a place for his chief wife and the Tyrian members of her court to worship their native god. But Ahab, it appears, intended this temple to be the central national shrine for the Canaanites in his territory. From this bright new capital Canaanite officials went about their government business, not always with enough regard for Israelite traditions, and tension turned into conflict, and at times became persecution.

That too is how a modern historian might talk of the reign of Ahab. The account of 1 Kings is more startling, much more one-sided, much more dramatic and exciting. It is unashamedly devoted to the high art of storytelling, and its theology is compelling.

The first contest

The most powerful and majestic human figure on its stage is not the king, nor the ruthless queen, but Elijah. He prowls around like a roaring lion, seeking whom he may devour, and woe betide Ahab if he should meet him in the slippery corridors of power! No sooner has he appeared than he introduces himself to us and to Ahab with a terrible oath: 'As the Lord the God of Israel lives, before whom I stand, there shall be neither dew nor rain these years, except by my word' (1 Kings 17.1). It is fearful not only for the obvious reason that it predicts complete and prolonged drought. It also reminds Ahab, the husband of Jezebel and builder of the Baal temple in Canaanite Samaria, who it is who is God in his kingdom, and who it is who controls the forces of nature. Canaanite religion, including the worship of the Tyrian Baal, had as one of its most important elements fertility ritual designed to ensure the coming of the rains, and the rebirth of the vegetation scorched to nothing by the summer sun. Elijah's words condemn Baal and the other Canaanite gods as powerless in this very sphere where they were thought to exercise such control. And they make further claims also. When Elijah describes himself as the one who 'stands before' Yahweh, he uses a phrase that was applied to the chief minister of the king. Thus he calls himself God's Prime Minister, and in doing so makes clear where his allegiance lies. Ahab cannot count on his loyalty. To the king's nostrils the words of the oath smell of treachery.

That would seem to be the prelude to conflict, and so it is, but the storyteller keeps us on tenterhooks for some while. We are not even allowed to wait for Ahab's response to the oath, but are off at God's command, hiding with Elijah in a remote wadi east of the Jordan. There God arranges for food and water to be supplied, until the drought that has indeed struck the land comes to the wadi and the stream disappears (17.2–7). Then Elijah must be on his way again, but not back to Ahab's centres of power. At God's bidding he crosses the country from east to west and ends up outside Israel altogether, at the town of Zarephath on the Phoenician coast, just twelve miles north of Tyre. Far from Samaria and Jezreel, still following God's directions, he lodges with the utterly powerless, a widow and her young son caught in the drought, and preparing to eat their last meal and die. Their hospitality is their salvation. Close to the heart of the territory of Jezebel's Baal, Elijah brings God's power to bring life, not only into the midst of starvation, but into the woman's bitter grief when, though saved from hunger, her son becomes ill and dies. Miraculously her jar of meal and cruse of oil replenish themselves, and miraculously again Elijah brings the child back to life (17.8–24).

But we cannot be kept waiting for ever. The word comes from God to Elijah: 'Go, show yourself to Ahab; and I will send rain upon the earth' (18.1). Elijah must go back among the powerful, and we can ring the bell for the start of round one.

In fact the storyteller has not done yet with keeping us in suspense. The scene shifts to Samaria, itself hit severely by the drought, and we overhear Ahab instructing Obadiah, the minister of the royal palace and estates, to help him search for grazing good enough to keep his horses and mules alive (18.2–6). We learn something here to alarm us, and something also to give us hope. The narrator tells us that Jezebel has been systematically killing the prophets of Yahweh. He tells us too that Obadiah, so close to the king, and in such a prominent position in his court, is yet a fervent worshipper of Yahweh, and has hidden a hundred of his prophets in caves. It is clear that Elijah's life must be in danger as he returns from Zarephath. But it is also clear that he is not alone, and has at least one friend in high places.

The scene changes again. We are back with Elijah, now inside the kingdom. Yet he meets not Ahab, but Obadiah, scouring the countryside for green grass. 'Go, tell your lord, "Behold Elijah is here." ' With this imperious command he would send Obadiah on his way. There is another whiff of treachery in the air. Ahab may be Obadiah's lord, but he is not Elijah's, and Elijah himself plays the king's part, summoning Ahab to appear before him. Not surprisingly Obadiah is more than a little unnerved by the order. But his long complaint, his panic, the protestation of his loyalty to Yahweh, and his plea for clemency are dismissed by Elijah in an oath that reminds us of his opening words in this series of stories: 'As the Lord of hosts lives, before whom I stand, I will surely show myself to him today' (18.15). There can be no arguing with that.

So Obadiah delivers the summons, and the mighty Ahab obeys! At last we have the meeting we have been waiting for. Elijah carries with him God's good news that the end of the drought is nigh. But Ahab's opening does not give him a chance to deliver it (18.17). The king greets him as the 'ruin of Israel' (the Hebrew is more forceful than the 'troubler' or 'troublemaker' of our versions). To this Elijah replies, not by telling him of the end of the drought, but by accusing him and his father of bringing its ruination upon the land by their neglect of Yahweh's demands, and their worship of Baal. Still conscious that he wears the authority of God, he gives the king his orders: to assemble 'all Israel' and Jezebel's host of prophets on Mount Carmel. So begins one of the most colourful and famous episodes in Israel's story (18.20–46).

In many of its features we can catch clear echoes of the story of the Golden Calf in Exodus 32. All Israel is there, challenged by Elijah, as once they were by Moses, to renew their allegiance to Yahweh, and to renounce the worship of other gods. No king was present at Sinai, and Ahab does not feature in this episode until it is over. He is put in his place as an anonymous member of the crowd, with no special authority, no power to take any initiative. After the Golden Calf Moses made atonement for the people's sin (Exod. 32.30–32). Now on the Carmel ridge Elijah would make atonement for the people's neglect of Yahweh under Omri and Ahab by sacrificing a bull.

But the sacrifice has layers of meaning beyond atonement. First, the bull can remind the people of the bull calf their ancestors made at Sinai. Secondly, it is for them one of the most powerful symbols of Canaanite religion. The father of the Canaanite gods was called 'Bull El' in its myths, and Baal, El's son, was himself sometimes called 'the Bull', and was pictured with bull's horns upon his head. The animal's strength and sexual potency was a sign, a reminder of the mighty Baal's ability to bring fertility to the land. When eventually the people on Carmel witness the bull on Elijah's altar going up in smoke, destroyed by Yahweh's lightning, they are witnesses to the end of Baal, as once the Philistines of Ashdod saw the end of Dagon.

The method of his destruction further reminds the people of the Golden Calf, for that too was destroyed by fire (Exod. 32.20), and it also underlines the completeness of Yahweh's victory. Baal, the rider of the clouds, the master of the storm, was celebrated as lord of thunder and lightning. When earlier in the story his own prophets, all 450 of them, call upon him for hours upon end to send the lightning and burn up the bull they have prepared for sacrifice on their own altar, they hear nothing but the taunts of Elijah. There is no rumble of thunder, no lightning, no sign of the coming of storm and the salvation of rain. It is Yahweh's drought, and Baal remains powerless to alter things. When Elijah calls on Yahweh, without the limping dance, the ecstatic trance, or the self-mutilation of the Baal prophets, but with a simple plea for him to act and show himself as God, then at once the lightning strikes, and soon clouds are seen massing over the Mediterranean, and the rain falls in torrents. The people prostrate themselves in worship of Yahweh, and Ahab returns in his chariot, not to Samaria, with its temple to the defeated Baal, but to Jezreel, where he can be an Israelite and not a Canaanite king.

Before he does so there is one more reminder of the story of the Golden Calf. Exodus 32 speaks of Moses calling upon the Levites to bring slaughter among those who had worshipped the Calf. So Elijah on Carmel orders the people to seize the prophets of Baal and kill them. Carmel ends up a darker place than Abraham's mountain in the land of Moriah, where also God's bounty was celebrated. There only the ram was burned. Here the bull is not enough. Suddenly, despite Elijah's ready ear for the word of God, Genesis seems a world away.

The second contest

Yahweh's and Elijah's victories sound comprehensive enough, but there remains one person to be reckoned with. Jezebel does not witness the events of Carmel. When Ahab tells her of them, her response sends shivers up the great Elijah's spine, and puts in train a series of events that are the concern of the first of the passages chosen for detailed comment in this chapter. But before we come to that, we must look for a moment at a story that appears a little later in the Elijah series, and which records a second occasion on which he and Ahab come into direct conflict with one another. It takes up the whole of chapter 21, and is the story of Naboth's vineyard.

The scene is set in the Israelite capital, Jezreel. Naboth, the hero of the story, until Elijah appears, is head of a prominent family in the city, which claims to be able to trace its ancestry back to the days of the occupation of the land, and its division among the tribes. So, at least, the details of the story would seem to imply. His family land is a vineyard, which happens to abut Ahab's palace complex. The king has plans for expansion, and offers to buy the vineyard, or give him another one for it. Naboth answers him in the strongest possible terms: 'The Lord forbid that I should give you the inheritance of my fathers' (21.3). Ahab has told him that he wants to turn the vineyard into a vegetable garden, but Naboth does not protest that those plans would ruin years of careful labour. In his view the land was given to his ancestors by God when the tribes settled in the country, and given to them in perpetuity, and that alone is enough to settle the matter. By asking to buy it from him, or exchange it for another plot, Ahab is asking him to hand over a sacred gift, and to sever his family's links with Israel's journey from bondage in Egypt to the freedom and security of the Promised Land.

Ahab submits to the higher power of Naboth's faith, and goes away disconsolate. When Jezebel finds him sulking to the point of refusing food, and asks the reason, he tells her half the truth about the transaction. What he omits to mention is the reason Naboth gave for not being willing to part with his land. He presents the affair as a straightforward business deal, in which he has been defeated. Jezebel herself enquires no further, but gives her husband a sharp reminder and a promise. She reminds him that he is king in Israel, and she promises that she will get the vineyard for him (21.7).

What follows is a brilliantly written tale of abuse of power (21.8–16). Jezebel well understands Israelite society and its workings, and she uses this knowledge and her ruthless cunning to get Naboth falsely charged, condemned and stoned to death by his fellow citizens. The vineyard is free now for Ahab's taking, and when Jezebel brings him the news, he does not hesitate.

But that is not the end of it. Elijah hears the news also, from God himself, and with it a commission to confront the king and pass God's judgement upon him. We have not heard of Elijah and Ahab coming across one another since Carmel. Now they meet again, at the scene of the crime, as Ahab is in the middle of taking possession of the vineyard. 'Have you found me, O my enemy?' asks the king. Before, he called him 'the ruin of Israel'. This time he sees the prophet more narrowly as the opponent of his personal ambitions. He is right, of course, or nearly so. His true enemy is God, who will not have such ruthless abuse of power in his Land. He will not allow Ahab and his queen to go on playing at being Canaanite tyrants in the midst of his people. He will rid himself of them once and for all, as mercilessly as they rid themselves of Naboth. So Elijah pronounces God's awful judgement upon them, and the first book of Kings closes with an account of Ahab's death in battle, while 2 Kings 9 gives us the gory tale of the death of Jezebel.

God's hero becomes God's fool

In each of these stories we have looked at, Elijah appears the master of the situation, or rather the one who exercises the unassailable mastery of God. In the Genesis—Kings narrative we have not seen a hero of God quite like this since Moses.

But we have already seen how that same narrative can bring its heroes down to earth. Abraham is taken for a ride by a clever Hittite, Jacob's extraordinary feat at the Jabbok is answered by his inability to come to terms with the magnanimity of his brother, and even Moses' faith in God's power to save his people fails at one point and results in his dying outside the Promised Land. Chapter 19 of 1 Kings furnishes us with yet another example of the storyteller's and compiler's mischief, another sign of their determination to save us from the attempt to make gods out of human beings.

The chapter begins, as we have already indicated, with Ahab telling Jezebel what has happened on Carmel. The emphasis of his report sounds ominous. He makes no mention of God, but tells her all that Elijah has done, and in particular how he has slaughtered all her precious prophets of Baal. Jezebel at once goes into action. If she complains first to the king, and demands an explanation of his failure to take control in the affair, we do not hear about it. What we do hear of is her sending a messenger to Elijah with an oath as fearful in its way as his to Ahab at the start of the drought: 'So may the gods do to me, and more also, if I do not make your life as the life of one of them by this time tomorrow.' By 'them' she means the slaughtered prophets of Baal. Elijah is terrified and turns to flight. He escapes first to Beer-sheba in the far south of Judah, and from there continues south into the desert.

This is the first time we have seen Elijah afraid, and the first time we have seen him acting solely on his own initiative. When he hid himself east of the Jordan after his initial encounter with Ahab, he did so at God's bidding. God it was also who sent him from there to Zarephath, who directed him towards the second meeting with the king that led to Carmel, and who will in chapter 21 tell him to find Ahab in Naboth's vineyard. Hitherto he has gone as God's diplomat, secure in his diplomatic immunity, and he will do so again. But this time he acts on his own impulse, and seeks to exercise his own mastery. He is about to be taught not to be so foolish.

At Beer-sheba he leaves his servant behind. This unnamed servant has already made a brief appearance at the end of the Carmel story (18.43–4). Here, no sooner is he mentioned than he leaves the stage, and we do not hear of him again. Nevertheless, he performs an important function in the story. He helps us feel more keenly how alone Elijah is as he goes on into the dangers of the wilderness. We may recall Abraham leaving his servants behind near the foot of the mountain in the land of Moriah, and going on alone with his son towards the horror of the sacrifice, or Jacob sending his entourage ahead across the Jabbok, and facing the dangers of a night crossing on his own.

Elijah goes a day's journey into the desert, and sitting in the shade of a broom tree, he reaches the end of his tether. 'Would that we had died in the land of Egypt! Or would that we had died in this wilderness!' cried the people of God on their journey in the desert (Num. 14.2; see also Exod. 16.3 and Num. 20.3). 'Enough! Now, O Lord, take away my life; for I am no better than my fathers,' exclaims Elijah. All the faith of Zarephath, the authority and assurance of Carmel, and the majestic anger with which he will meet Ahab in the vineyard, are nowhere to be found in this wilderness. He is no roaring lion here, and Ahab can for the moment rest easy on his bed.

Who does Elijah mean by his 'fathers'? We cannot be sure, but in these circumstances we cannot help but think of those generations of Israelites in this story who have already caused God such pain, and in particular of that most fickle generation that came out of Egypt and in the desert was so quick to despair. Certainly we must think of them when we learn of the response to Elijah's cry. He lies down to sleep, hoping, as many have done, not to wake up in the morning.

But he is aroused by someone touching him, and by the words, 'Arise and eat.' As Israel's despair in the wilderness on the way to Sinai was answered at once by acts of salvation, and the people's hunger and thirst satisfied by manna and quails and sweet water, so Elijah's hopelessness is met with the gift of a cooked breakfast.

Here we meet another uncertainty. The Hebrew word used for the bringer of the meal can mean 'angel', as our English versions have it, but it is also the usual term for 'messenger'. Curiously enough, when Elijah was provided with food in the wadi east of the Jordan, the Hebrew left it uncertain whether his immediate helpers were ravens or Arabs (17.4–6; the RSV and the rest opt for ravens). In the case of chapter 19 we are tempted to trust the translations, and to recall how the story of the exodus from Egypt speaks of God as an angel accompanying his people (Exod. 14.19), and how the story of the binding of Isaac has God intervene at the crucial moment as an angel from heaven. At least we must recognize that, whether God himself or a human messenger from God, Elijah's saviour comes with divine insight into Elijah's need, with divine timing, and with a divine twinkle in the eye. Gently, as we can see in the Hebrew, he mocks Elijah's words and actions. Without a word of gratitude or surprise Elijah eats the breakfast, but that is not enough to shake him out of his despair. He 'returns' to sleep, but his saviour then 'returns' to touch him awake again and to bid him eat a second meal. 'Arise and eat,' he says, 'else the journey will be too great for you.' The Hebrew word translated 'too great' is the same as the 'enough' of Elijah's opening cry of despair.

Still no surprise, no cry of 'The Lord provides!', no giving of a name like Peniel to the place. But at least now Elijah resumes his journey, and sustained by that food for 'forty days and forty nights', as the Israelites were fed by the manna for forty years (Exod. 16.35), where does he go but Sinai, called in this particular story by its alternative name of Horeb! He is playing the role of the Israel of the exodus for all it's worth!

Once at the mountain he changes his costume, and plays Moses as he did on Mount Carmel. God, with an even brighter twinkle in his eye, as we shall see, decides to go along with him.

In Exodus 33, so soon after the terrible story of the Golden Calf, we come across a brief passage that is surely one of the great treasures of the Bible (vv. 18–23). Moses, who has already spent so long talking with God 'face to face, as a man speaks to his friend', strangely asks God to show him his glory. When he does not ask, he comes down from the mountain with his face shining so brightly, that the people and his own brother are afraid to come near him (Exod. 34.29–30). When he does ask, he presumes too much. In effect he bids to rob the encounter of its naturalness, its glorious ordinariness and matter-of-factness that comes straight from Eden, and which, ironically, he in this narrative is the last to enjoy. Nevertheless, God does not refuse him outright, but tells him to 'stand upon the rock', and then, hiding him in a cleft and shielding him with his hand, he passes him by in the full glory of his goodness and mercy, taking his hand away as he retreats so that Moses can see his back. We have to hold this story in our minds as we come back to 1 Kings 19, together with the account of God's first coming to Sinai with thunder and lightning, thick cloud, loud trumpet blast, and the fire and smoke of earthquake, to deliver his torah to his people (Exod. 19.16ff.).

When he reaches Sinai/Horeb, Elijah finds a cave and spends the night there, hidden, like Moses, in a cleft in the rock. Now, for the first time in this story, 'the word of the Lord' finds him (the words of the 'angel' or 'messenger' are not accorded that sonorous title). It is hardly surprising that it should come to him in this particular place. What is surprising, however, is its extreme brevity and its content: 'What are you doing here, Elijah?' The question has a tone of surprise about it. What else it contains, whether anger or amusement, we shall have to wait and see, though we might do well to remember the mischievous mimicry of the mysterious visitor in the desert.

Elijah does not give God a direct answer, but the question is enough to release his bitterness and despair. 'I have been very jealous for the Lord, the God of hosts; for the people of Israel have forsaken thy covenant, thrown down thy altars, and slain thy prophets with the sword; and I, even I only, am left; and they seek my life, to take it away.' It is in several ways a strange speech. It seems that his fear has led him to get things quite out of perspective. He makes no mention of Jezebel or the oath of hers that sent him running. Instead he makes 'the people of Israel' into the villains of the piece. At one point he echoes words he spoke on Mount Carmel, when he said to the people, 'I, even I only, am left a prophet of the Lord' (18.22). Those words were somewhat ungracious, in that they ignored the hundred prophets of Yahweh hidden in caves by Obadiah. But Elijah *was* the only prophet of Yahweh on Carmel, and his words were clearly designed to add to the drama of the occasion,

and eventually to highlight the power of a God who needed the
resources of but one prophet in order to do his work. Now, on Sinai,
his 'I, even I only, am left', a much more extreme statement than
before, with its omission of the phrase 'a prophet of the Lord', at first
sight makes no sense at all. For did not 'all Israel' prostrate
themselves on Carmel and cry, 'The Lord, he is God; the Lord, he is
God!' (18.39)?

Yet God does not remonstrate with Elijah or correct his account.
Instead he prepares him, or seems to prepare him, for a grand
theophany. 'Go forth, and stand upon the mount before the Lord,'
he tells him. It is just like his command to Moses in Exodus 33.
Next, as we and Elijah might expect, he passes by in a wind that
breaks the rocks in pieces, in earthquake, then in fire. But here we
discover the second of this God's surprises. He is not in the wind,
nor the earthquake, nor the fire. The phenomena which in Exodus
19 accompanied his first appearance on Sinai were indeed the off-
shinings of his glory. This wind, this earthquake, and this fire are
but empty show. They are tricks, a joke, gently beneath their noise
still poking fun at God's favourite fool.

The joke would be cruel if that was the end of it, but everybody
knows that it is not. Everybody knows, or thinks they know, what
comes next: 'a still small voice'. But that famous translation of the
King James Version, retained by the RSV, is an attempt to make
sense of some ambiguous Hebrew, and probably makes a mess of
things. There are three Hebrew words to be dealt with, the first
meaning 'sound' or 'voice', the second meaning 'silence' (it comes
from a verb that means 'to be or grow still, silent, dumb') and the
third meaning 'thin', 'small', 'fine'. Put together, what they most
probably mean is 'the sound of utter silence', and what they
probably refer to is not the point of divine revelation itself, but the
awesome moment immediately before it, when all creation seems to
hold its breath. Translated in that way they certainly help to explain
what happens next, and they allow our concentration to fall on what
is undoubtedly the true climax of the story.

When Elijah catches the mysterious silence, he wraps his face in
his cloak and goes to the entrance of the cave. Like Moses at the
Burning Bush, he hides his face, presumably because he is afraid to
look upon God (see Exod. 3.6). His doing so and his going to the
mouth of the cave, are not the actions of one who has just received a
revelation of God, but of one who, disappointed by the wind,
earthquake and fire, now expects to receive one.

A revelation of a kind is precisely what he is given, but it is hardly what he has been expecting, or what any hearer of the story could anticipate. It is the third and the greatest of God's surprises. Elijah has no vision granted him, but instead he hears 'a voice'. The storyteller does not say whose voice it is, meaning no doubt to add a last pinch of mystery to his account. But Elijah and we know well enough the identity of the speaker. It is the same one as has been playing with him all along. So the 'voice' speaks . . . and utters exactly the same question as before, 'What are you doing here, Elijah?'!

If we refuse or do not expect to find any humour in the Bible, we will miss the brilliance of this climax to the story. If we are prepared to laugh, then we may agree that this is one of the funniest moments in all Scripture, and declare the storyteller an assured master of the anticlimax.

Nor has he finished with his humour. Elijah does not get the joke! Hearing the same question again, he gives the same reply, word for word! 'I have been very jealous for the Lord . . .' We can only suppose he thinks God did not hear him the first time.

But we must not laugh again so hard that we miss what Elijah is saying. His words remain utterly serious, and his seriousness invites us to look again at the question God has put to him. Why *is* he there? Why has he come to Sinai/Horeb in particular? Not simply to play Moses again, and to have a chance to play the Israel of the exodus along the way, that is for sure. A man of his seriousness is doing more than play-acting. To meet with God, then? But he has seemed to enjoy such a close relationship with him, and if, despite that, he needed to find holy ground far from Jezebel, why did he not choose one of the sanctuaries of Judah? Is it, perhaps, that he is inviting God to start all over again? During the incident of the Golden Calf God threatened, as we saw in chapter 4, to destroy Israel altogether and create a new people from the descendants of Moses (Exod. 32.10). As we also saw, he repeated that threat, or made one very similar, in the complaint story of Numbers 14 (v. 12). Is Elijah now, with his strange, twice repeated 'I, even I only, am left', trying to remind God of his twice-made threat, and trying to suggest to him that at the place that marked the beginnings of Israel as his people, he must indeed begin again with him? If so, then his desperation is not all it seems, but hides a vast ambition to alter the course of history, and to change the direction of God's plans to redeem his creation. If so, then the time for laughter is at an end, and God must stop playing and give him an answer to match his seriousness.

Certainly that is what he does. He gives Elijah a threefold commission, a threefold prediction, and an assurance. His fool must stop playing Moses and a new Israel. Instead he must go far to the north, to the wilderness of Damascus, and there he must anoint Hazael king over Syria. In the kingdom of Israel he must make Jehu king, and he must anoint Elisha as his own successor. Hazael will bring terrible slaughter to Israel, and Jehu will continue it, leaving Elisha to finish things off. But in the end there will be a remnant of seven thousand left who will have remained loyal to God.

There is no laughter now. This God, like Elijah, is in deadly earnest. No matter that, as things turn out, Elijah only fulfils the third of his tasks. Israel will indeed suffer grievously at the hands of Hazael, and Jehu will come to power through a blood-bath; and though, mercifully, we hear of no massacre brought about by Elisha, those who first heard the Kings narrative could well have identified themselves as God's remnant, left after the ruthless campaigns of the Babylonians. This divine 'torah', delivered to Elijah from the summit of Sinai, will fit events well enough.

It is clear what God has done. He has rejected Elijah's romantic plans. He has corrected his illusion, or devious claim, whichever it is, that he is on his own. He has shown him that his own commitment to his people and to his ugly and violent world will not be shaken, and he has sent him back into the thick of it, to play his part there again as his diplomat. Elijah does not disappoint him. Though he will have to leave the king-making to Elisha, soon he will be heading for a vineyard in Jezreel, and a king who has been made to forget again, even after Carmel, who is truly Lord in Israel.

Elisha and Naaman: setting the scene

To set the scene for the story of 2 Kings 5 will not take very long. Though the stories of Elijah we have looked at arose independently of one another, they have been skilfully put together by the compiler to form a connected narrative. To get deep into the story of the journey to Sinai/Horeb, it was necessary to examine the Elijah stories on either side of it. The Elisha stories, however, which begin in earnest in 2 Kings 2, are much more of a motley collection. The story of Elisha and Naaman stands to a large extent on its own. Though it refers to 'the king of Syria' and 'the king of Israel', for example, it is not concerned to tie the story to the surrounding material by identifying who they are.

There are just four things we should have in our minds as we approach the story, three concerning Elisha himself, and one concerning the times in which he lived.

Chapter 3 of 2 Kings tells of a campaign against the kingdom of Moab undertaken by the kings of Israel, Judah, and Edom. At one point in their advance their forces run desperately short of water, and the three kings seek a prophet who with his divine insight might tell them how to find some, and who might also predict the outcome of their venture. They turn to Elisha, but the king of Israel, who is the spokesman for them all, does not receive a friendly welcome (vv. 13–14). 'What have I to do with you?' is Elisha's greeting. 'Go to the prophets of your father and the prophets of your mother' (by which he means Ahab's and Jezebel's prophets of Baal). The king protests his faith in Yahweh, and Elisha agrees to help, albeit grudgingly. 'As the Lord of hosts lives, before whom I stand, were it not that I have regard for Jehoshaphat the king of Judah, I would neither look at you, nor see you.' Except for the fact that he gives God a different title, and calls him 'the Lord of hosts', Elisha introduces himself with the same words as Elijah used to Ahab in 1 Kings 17.1. He is Yahweh's first minister, and owes no loyalty to the king. Two things are clear about him from this episode: like Elijah he walks the corridors of power, and like Elijah also, he is no respecter of persons.

The Elisha stories on either side of the account of the Moabite war, in the second half of chapter 2 and throughout chapter 4, present him not as a remonstrator with kings, but as a wonder-worker. There is, indeed, no wonder-worker to compare with Elisha anywhere else in the Old Testament. That is the third thing to remember about him as we come to the story of Naaman.

Chapter 19 of 1 Kings, which ends with Elisha's call, is followed by an account of war between Israel and Syria, of Samaria besieged, and then of a great slaughter of Syrian troops, of battle joined a second time, and the Syrians defeated even more comprehensively (ch. 20). This is not the first we have heard of conflict between the two kingdoms, for a passage in 1 Kings 15 describes the Syrians invading and conquering part of Israel. Chapter 22 begins with three years of peace between the two peoples, but then war breaks out again, and this time victory falls to the Syrians, and Ahab is killed in battle. In 2 Kings 6, almost immediately after the end of the Naaman story, the story of conflict with Syria is resumed, and together with chapter 7 it traces the course of a much longer and more terrible siege of Samaria. Though the city survives, it is still not the end of the story, and accounts of Israel, and Judah also, at war with Syria, continue to appear in the narrative until chapter 16, by which time a much larger and more terrible foe, Assyria, has come on the scene. If Philistia was the most powerful enemy of the Israelites in the period of Eli and Samuel, undoubtedly Syria is the arch enemy of Israel at the time of Elisha. This is the fourth item on our list, and the most important to remember as we enter 2 Kings 5. The story begins by reminding us of it, but after that we will have to remember it for ourselves.

A general, a slave girl, and dealings between kings

Elisha does not appear in the story for some time, but Naaman is introduced right at the start, and the terms of his introduction are of the utmost importance. 'Naaman, commander of the army of the king of Syria . . . a great man with his master and in high favour, because by him the Lord had given victory to Syria . . . mighty man of valour, leper.' He comes from the heart of the enemy camp, and has recently inflicted the suffering of war and the bitterness of defeat upon Israel. Though we are told next to nothing about his campaign, his success has been enough to give great satisfaction to his king, and establish him as a powerful and influential man in the court. The mention of Yahweh as having brought him victory may startle us, but we saw in the story of the capture of the ark the way in which Israelite monotheism led Israel to ascribe her defeats as well as her victories to the might of her own God. Thus, step by step the storyteller builds up such a fine picture of the man, and then with one word (the Hebrew is more abrupt than our usual English versions) he shatters it: *leper*!

Modern commentators tell us that 'leper' is something of a misnomer, that true leprosy probably did not reach the Near East till some of Alexander the Great's soldiers returned with it from India, and that the term 'leprosy' is used in the Old Testament to cover what was probably a variety of disfiguring skin diseases. But the nice distinctions of modern diagnosis matter little as far as this and other biblical stories of 'lepers' are concerned. In all of them the seriousness of the disease is clear, and it is plain also that recovery or cure was rare, and that sufferers were often ostracized from their families and their communities. In the story of the siege of Samaria in 2 Kings 6–7 we hear of four lepers condemned to a life of sitting outside the city gates, begging from those who might come in and out – not the best place to be in a siege, one might think, though for them there is a delicious twist in the tale (but that is another story, to be found in 7.3ff).

However, when you are in Naaman's position and contract leprosy, you do not find yourself begging at the city gates, but your king writes a letter for you, and you go abroad to the best physician, or rather, since this is the Ancient Near East, the best prophet or wonder-worker that money can buy. So eventually Naaman comes to Elisha's door in Samaria.

But before he gets there, we are treated to some gentle satire. Naaman hears of Elisha from a small Israelite girl, captured on one of the Syrian raids, and now slave to his wife. She tells her mistress of 'the prophet who is in Samaria' who would cure Naaman of his disease. The mistress tells Naaman, who tells the king, who does what a king might be expected to do, even outside peace time: he packs his commander off to Samaria with a quite enormous bribe, and sends ahead of him a letter addressed to the king of Israel, declaring that he has sent Naaman that he might cure him of his leprosy. It is perfectly plain to us, as it would have been plain to the first hearers of the story, that this is the courteous language of diplomacy. Everyone knows that the king is not expected to effect the cure himself; everyone supposes that the Syrian king assumes Naaman will be sent on to 'the prophet who is in Samaria'; everyone realizes that the subsequent cure will be sure to redound to the king of Israel's credit, and that it will most likely be *said* that he cured the general himself. Powerful people are often said to have done things when they did not lift a finger. Everyone understands. Everyone, that is, except the king of Israel! The letter sends him into a blind panic. Taking its terms literally, and thinking the king of Syria is deliberately asking the impossible, he believes he is seeking a pretext for another invasion. The contrast between the wisdom of a little slave girl and the frantic idiocy of her king is marvellous to behold!

The beginning, the middle, and the end of Naaman's cure

It is conceivable that the story could have ended there, but, of course, it has only just begun. Elisha hears of the king's alarm. Whether he has heard the gossip of the court, or has relied on supernatural insight, is left for us to decide, but he immediately saves the situation by telling the king to send Naaman to him. 'Let him come now to me,' he says, 'that he may know that there is a prophet in Israel.' Naaman has come to Israel to get his leprosy cured. Elisha means not only to cure him, but to teach him a lesson.

Naaman does not get what he bargained for. Driving through the streets of this enemy capital with the freedom of the victorious general that he is, he arrives at Elisha's door in his chariot, with his servants beside him. There he stands at the gate of the house, waiting for Elisha to come out, as the four lepers of chapter 7 will wait at the gate of the city. But Elisha does not come. His off-handedness provides us with another delicious contrast with the consternation of the king. He sends a messenger. No doubt that is precisely what Naaman would have done in Elisha's shoes. With a leper waiting outside his door, he would have sent a messenger. As a general and as a fine man at court, he must have been used to sending messengers to people he preferred not to deal with himself. But fine men are not used to being treated as they treat their subordinates, let alone by one who belongs to a defeated enemy people. Naaman, understandably, is angry. And the content of the message adds considerably to his anger: 'Go and wash in the Jordan seven times, and your flesh will be restored, and you will be clean.' That is all. No pomp, no circumstance, no ceremony large enough to stand on. The requirements in Israel concerning not the cure of a leper, but merely the ritual cleansing once the disease had gone, were immensely complicated (see Lev. 14.1–32). They included the sprinkling of water seven times, and bathing in water (Lev. 14.7,9), to be sure, but they involved so much more, and they ensured the job was done properly, and seen to be done. Some of the original hearers of the story may themselves have been shocked by the simplicity of Elisha's remedy. Certainly Naaman expected much more, and paying no heed to the assurances of a cure attached to Elisha's instruction, he turns on his heel and goes away in high dudgeon.

Once again the story might have ended there, but just as a slave girl pointed Naaman in Elisha's direction in the first place, so now his servants urge him to follow Elisha's instructions. They clearly understand their master well. They know that if the holy man had required him to do something much more demanding, he would have done it. He would have risen to the challenge, and would have derived some satisfaction out of the exercise, beyond the cure itself. He would have achieved a sense that he had *done* something, and he would have been able secretly to congratulate himself. They understand, these anonymous Syrians, that Elisha has been trying to teach their master a lesson in humility.

To his great credit Naaman is persuaded by them. He learns Elisha's lesson. It is the start of his cure.

The middle part of his healing is described in a single sentence. He goes to the Jordan, dips himself in it seven times, and comes out of the water with his flesh like that of 'a little child'. We are reminded of that other little child, with whom the story began, and of her wisdom and simplicity. This indeed is the cure of one who has learned Elisha's lesson. But Elisha has not yet finished with teaching.

Naaman returns to him from the Jordan. That in itself is remarkable. The Jordan at its closest point was more than a day's journey from Samaria, and the city was not at all on the direct way home. Damascus lay to the north-east. To reach Elisha again, Naaman has had to travel west. He arrives with his entourage, but not with airs and graces any more. He is cured of his pride as well as his leprosy, and there is no need now for Elisha to keep his distance. For the first time the two men meet one another, and Naaman at once acknowledges Elisha's greater authority: he 'stands before' him and calls himself his 'servant'. Now he offers him the vast hoard of gold and silver and fine garments he has brought with him. He no longer offers them as a bribe, for the leprosy is gone, but as he might offer tribute to a great king. But he extends to him also a confession of faith: 'Behold, I know that there is no God in all the earth but in Israel'. In his earlier message to the king of Israel Elisha said, 'Let him come now to me, that he may know that there is a prophet in Israel.' Naaman has learned more quickly than Elisha anticipated. He has not just found a prophet in Israel, he has found a God.

But there is a contradiction in his speech which Elisha must expose in order to complete his cure. If he found God himself, why does he offer his tribute to the prophet? Elisha reminds him that he himself 'stands before' God (the phrase in the Hebrew of verse 16 is the same as that used of Naaman in verse 15, and the same as Elisha used in 2 Kings 3.14, and Elijah in 1 Kings 17.1), and stubbornly refuses to take anything. Naaman, to his continuing credit, learns his final lesson. He will offer his gifts to the one who deserves them, to God himself, and not the treasures he brought with him from Damascus, but gifts of burnt offering and sacrifice. Instead of giving anything to Elisha, he asks for something from him. He knows that God is God of 'all the earth', yet he recognizes that Israel is his Land, and he wishes to establish an 'embassy' for him in Damascus, a small patch of his sovereign territory. He puts away his gold and silver and fine garments, and requests two loads of soil.

He remains commander of the Syrian army, and a great man at the court of Damascus. He knows he will have to accompany his king into the temple of his god, and keep up appearances of worship. He understands the compromises, the deceit that power and privilege will demand of him. And as he talks of this and asks God's pardon, his speech takes on the formality and uneasy courtesy of the court. It is a wonderful example of the storyteller's art. His first confession was so simple, and uncluttered. His second speech is repetitious, pompous and awkward. But Elisha does not criticize this pupil who has learned so much. Instead he answers his anxiety with a simple 'Go in peace', and with those words declares the cure complete, and the ceremonies of his cleansing fulfilled. Naaman goes on his way.

Lessons from an enemy

Naaman's startling confession of faith in God is reminiscent of the cry of the people on Carmel, 'The Lord, he is God; the Lord he is God.' It is similar also to declarations made in prayer by David (2 Sam. 7.22), and Solomon (1 Kings 8.23). But the David of humble prayer is soon followed in the narrative by the David who abuses his power most cruelly to satisfy his lust (see 2 Sam. 11), and Solomon sinks to tyranny. As for the people of Carmel, if we can believe the claims of Elijah at Sinai at all, then their loyalty to God was washed away in the rains that broke the drought. Like Abraham, like Jacob, like Elijah himself, those two fine kings and 'all Israel' on Carmel are sent flying off their pedestals. In the final scene of this story, however, Naaman, the enemy commander, is further exalted. It is not that he does anything more that is outstandingly admirable, but the new picture of him is sustained, and thrown into sharper relief by the greed and duplicity of Elijah's Israelite servant.

Gehazi has already featured in two of the miracle stories of chapter 4. We see there that he did not possess his master's insight or supernatural power, but he does not appear in an especially bad light. Chapter 4 does not prepare us for the end of chapter 5. Angry that Elisha has sent Naaman on his way back to Damascus with his bags of silver and gold and fine garments still intact, he runs after him, makes up a story about his master needing to have something to give two unexpected guests, pushes his luck by begging a huge present, takes the spoils back to Elisha's house, hides them, and then, when challenged by Elisha, denies having done anything. The episode borders on comedy, but its conclusion is not comic. Elisha, who knows exactly what Gehazi has been up to, and what he plans to do with the great bags of silver he has hidden, pronounces disquieting judgement upon him, and leaves him and his descendants with something else that Naaman brought from Syria, his leprosy.

We might think that Naaman is made to look a fool by Gehazi. This powerful man, so wise, surely, in the ways of the world, so realistic, certainly, about his own situation, is seemingly taken in by a greedy rogue. But we are not told he believes Gehazi's story. We are told he gets down from his chariot to meet him, and we are told he gives him nearly double what he asks for, but that is all. Whether he is naïve or not is left for us to decide, but the absence of the pride with which he came to Israel and his great generosity are put beyond doubt. Moreover, his new-found faith now shines more brightly against the dark cloud of Gehazi's obtuseness. 'Was it a time to accept money and garments. . . ?' Elisha asks Gehazi. When Elisha refused his gifts, Naaman learned the lesson being taught about the grace and the generosity of God. Gehazi obviously did not even see what his master was trying to teach.

Throughout the story Elisha is teacher, Naaman the pupil. But for those who first heard the story being read Naaman must have ended up the teacher, and must have given them a lesson they found hard to forget.

Exodus 18, after the first series of the people's complaints in the wilderness, and just before the great encounter with God on Sinai, describes a meeting between Moses and his father-in-law, Jethro. Jethro is not an Israelite, but a priest of the desert people of Midian. Yet when he hears of the coming out of Egypt, and the gifts of food and water in the wilderness, he at once rejoices, and declares, 'Blessed be the Lord, who has delivered you out of the hand of the Egyptians and out of the hand of Pharaoh. Now I know that the Lord is greater than all gods, because he delivered the people from under the hand of the Egyptians, when they dealt arrogantly with them.' The narrator continues, 'And Jethro, Moses' father-in-law, offered a burnt offering and sacrifices to God' (Exod. 18: 10–12).

The contrast between this Midianite's reaction to the events of the exodus and that of the Israelites of the complaint stories could not be clearer, nor more pointed. As the people go to Sinai, Jethro puts them to great shame, and teaches them how to begin to respond to their God, how to worship him and requite his love.

Naaman's confession of faith bears a remarkable similarity to part of Jethro's, and with him too there is talk of burnt offering and sacrifice. He is there in the midst of the narrative concerning the turbulent and faithless times of the monarchy, to encourage the same sense of shame, and to teach the same lesson. What is so very remarkable about 2 Kings 5 is that the one who teaches Israel is not only a foreigner like Jethro, but the army commander of her arch-enemy. As a story for those enduring defeat and exile under the Babylonians it is astonishing. Only one work in the Old Testament goes further still, and that is Jonah.

7

GOD'S FOOL II: this time in Berlin

(The Book of Jonah)

A giant of a little book

With the book of Jonah we step beyond the Genesis—Kings
narrative, though we do not leave it entirely behind. Jonah contains
many echoes of that narrative, some of passages of which we have
already explored. On the likes of the Jericho story it sits quietly in
judgement, and it leads us back towards where we began, with the
bright designs of God in his creation of the world and in the calling of
Abraham. It will leave us at the foot of the Cross.

It is impossible to date securely. Various attempts to attach it to a
particular century have depended too heavily on one reading or
another of the author's purpose, and are not easily to be trusted. It
appears to show knowledge of the preaching of Jeremiah, who lived
in Jerusalem at the time of the capture of Jerusalem, and most
scholars would place it after the period of the exile in Babylon.
Beyond that it is very difficult to go, and the effort is hardly worth
making. For whatever the times of its composition, Jonah
transcends them. Wherever men and women believe in God, and so
long as there is prejudice, fear, hatred and war in human society,
then Jonah will lose nothing of its ancient power. Like the creation
stories of Genesis 1 and 2–3, it is a story for all times and all peoples.

Impossible to date, it is also impossible to put firmly in one precise
literary category. Though not history, it is linked by the author to
historical events, and somewhat loosely to a particular historical
period. It has elements of fairy-tale and satire about it, but it cannot
properly be called either of those. It bears the clear marks of a
prophetic legend, a story about a prophet, like the stories of Elijah

and Elisha. But, despite its being placed among the prophetic books in our Bibles, it is not simply that. It is very nearly parable, and certainly some of its most important features are held in common with the parables of Jesus. But it is not quite that either. Undoubtedly it is story, and it is probably best to leave it at that and be glad of the very vagueness of the word, so long as we concede that a story can contain a poem, and, after our examination of stories from the Genesis—Kings narrative, agree that it can also have a profound and serious intent.

It is written with enormous care and precision. Every word of it counts, and perhaps at points its words were actually counted. Jonah's first speech in chapter 4 is made up of thirty-nine words in the Hebrew, and is 'answered' by a speech of God's which closes the book and which contains exactly thirty-nine words. Some of those are linked by a kind of hyphen called a *maqqeph*, which has the effect of making a pair of words into one. If we take the '*maqqephs*' into account, then each speech has thirty words.

Such precision could make for tediousness, but this storyteller writes with the lightest of touches. His work is full of wit and humour, and sometimes comes close to pantomime. He understands the art of gentle parody, and in that vein knows how to write poetry. He knows how to vary his pace, how to engage our sympathies, how to surprise, how, indeed, to shock without losing his audience. For Jonah is at once one of the most entertaining pieces of writing in the Bible, and one of the most disturbing. On one level it is just a good, though sometimes puzzling yarn. On another it is a work of the deepest seriousness, whose theology is in certain respects more audacious, perhaps, than anything else in the Bible outside the Passion Narratives of the Gospels. It can be enjoyed by children, yet demands of its adult readers great maturity of faith, and an unusual willingness to engage in adventure, not only in their thinking and believing, but in the whole of their living. On its deeper level Jonah is most decidedly not a work for the faint-hearted.

Nineveh and Jonah ben Amittai

Jonah begins with the words, 'Now the word of the Lord came to Jonah ben Amittai, saying, 'Arise, go to Nineveh . . .' Both Jonah ben Amittai and Nineveh belong to history, and we must take a brief look into the parts they play there before we enter the story. Without considering the significance of Nineveh, certainly, we cannot hope to feel the full force of the story's shock.

The city was the last capital of the Assyrian empire. The Assyrians are famed for the sculptured reliefs which once adorned the palaces of their kings. The reliefs of lion hunts to be found in the British Museum, for example, are among the finest depictions of animals in human art. But the Assyrians are even better known for their militarism, and for the terror they spread throughout the Ancient Near East when they held sway. Their armies were larger, their troops better organized and disciplined, their kings more ruthless in their ambitions than any seen in that part of the world before.

> None is weary, none stumbles,
>   none slumbers or sleeps,
> not a waistcloth is loose,
>   not a sandal-thong broken;
> their arrows are sharp,
>   all their bows bent,
> their horses' hoofs seem like flint,
>   and their wheels like the whirlwind.
> Their roaring is like a lion,
>   like young lions they roar;
> they growl and seize their prey,
>   they carry it off, and none can rescue.

That is how the prophet Isaiah described them in the eighth century BCE (Isa. 5.27–9). When in the following century their empire reached its greatest extent, they claimed control of the whole of the Mesopotamian region, a large area to the east of it, Egypt, all Palestine, Cyprus, and a considerable part of Asia Minor, of what is now southern Turkey.

They were masters of psychological warfare, adept at convincing other peoples of their invincibility, devastatingly quick to punish treachery or rebellion. Time and again their ruthlessness is the subject of their boasting in their royal annals.

At the end of the eighth century, Sargon II destroyed a herding centre at a certain Aniashtania, together with seventeen surrounding villages:

> I set fire to the long beams of their roofs. I burned up their harvest and their hay. I opened up their heaped-up granaries and let the troops eat corn unrationed. I turned the livestock of my

camp into its pastures like swarming locusts; they stripped off the grass on which the city relied, and devastated its meadowlands.

In the next century Ashurbanipal records a campaign to bring some Egyptian towns to heel: 'Tanis and all the other towns which had associated with them to plot, they' (that is his troops or generals) 'did not spare anybody among them. They hung their corpses from stakes, flayed their skins and covered with them the walls of the towns.' In another passage he describes a campaign against Arab tribes, and the measures he took against the fugitives who had escaped his onslaught in battle:

> I ordered soldiers to stand on guard in the towns . . . anywhere where there were cisterns or water in the springs . . . I thus made water to be very rare for their lips, and many perished of parching thirst. The others slit open camels, their only means of transportation, drinking blood and filthy water against their thirst. None of those who ascended the mountain or entered this region to hide there, did escape; none was fleet enough of foot to get out of my hands. I caught them all myself in their hiding-places; countless people – male and female – donkeys, camels, large and small cattle, I led away as booty to Assyria.

This third passage refers at the end to a policy which the Assyrians first put into practice in the thirteenth century BCE, that of deportation. In the last three centuries of their power they deported, according to some estimates, between four and five million people. In their conquered territories nothing was more destructive of national identity. Large sections of populations, and even larger sections of native ruling classes, were resettled far from their homelands. Their territories were turned into provinces of the empire, ruled by Assyrian governors and administrators. Sometimes conquered lands were left so depopulated, that very large numbers of people beyond the new ruling class were brought into them from other parts of the empire. Such was the fate of the northern kingdom of Israel, and nearly that of Judah also.

In 733 BCE, after devastating invasion and the destruction of many cities, most of Israel's territory became three Assyrian provinces, and the people had their first taste of deportation. Eleven years later, after another invasion and a siege lasting over two years, Samaria itself fell to Sargon II, and the city and its surrounding area was turned into a fourth province. The events are recorded in 2 Kings 15, 17, and 18, and their terror can be caught in the prophecies of Hosea. They spelled the end of Israel, and eventually gave rise to the talk of the 'ten lost tribes'.

Little Judah herself was punished for rebellion in 701. The Assyrian king, Sennacherib, with huge resources at his command, besieged and captured forty-six cities, took countless villages, and laid siege to Jerusalem itself. The city surrendered, and was stripped of its treasures. With parts of its territory lost altogether, with a large number of its people deported to Assyria, Judah lived on for another ninety years under Assyria's domination, until in 612 Nineveh fell to the Babylonians, and the cudgels of invasion and deportation were taken up by a second superpower.

In 2 Kings 18–19 we have an account, or rather three accounts blended into one, of the invasion of 701. Though it obscures the humiliation of Jerusalem, and the historical accuracy of its version of the end of the siege cannot be relied upon, it allows us to feel something of what the inhabitants of the cities must have felt as they surveyed the Assyrian troops surrounding their walls. But the Judaeans' bitterness and hatred of the Assyrians is most powerfully conveyed in the poems of the prophet Nahum, composed immediately before, or just after Nineveh's fall.

> Woe to the bloody city,
>   all full of lies and booty –
> no end to the plunder!
>
> Behold, I am against you,
>   says the Lord of hosts,
>   and will lift up your skirts over your face;
> and I will let nations look on your nakedness
>   and kingdoms on your shame.
> I will throw filth at you
>   and treat you with contempt,
>   and make you a gazingstock.   (Nahum 3.1, 5–6)

The book leaves Nineveh with a question:

> For upon whom has not come
>   your unceasing evil?   (3.19)

So much for Nineveh. As for the historical Jonah ben Amittai, he makes the briefest of appearances in the narrative of 2 Kings, where it is said that Jeroboam II, king of Israel, 'restored the border of Israel from the entrance of Hamath' (the northern limit of Solomon's kingdom) 'as far as the sea of the Arabah' (the Dead Sea), 'according to the word of the Lord, the God of Israel, which he spoke by his servant Jonah the son of Amittai, the prophet, who was from Gath-hepher' (2 Kings 14.25).

The significance of Nineveh in the book of Jonah is crystal clear. Though almost certainly the city had long gone by the time the work was written, it still represented for the Jew all that was evil in the pagan world, all that was brutal, ruthless and destructive. No other power had brought the Israelites such suffering, or caused such ruin among them. The book of Jonah is itself evidence that Nineveh occupied much the same place in the minds of Jews after the exile as is filled in the minds of contemporary Jews by Hitler's Berlin.

But if we ask why the storyteller named his hero after Jeroboam's Jonah, the answer is much harder to find. The ancient Israelites were fascinated by the meaning of names, and it may be that the author chose Jonah because his name meant 'dove', and Israel had been compared to a dove in one of the Psalms (74.19), and twice by Hosea (7.11 and 11.11). Undoubtedly the Jonah of the book does represent Israel, and with Amittai meaning 'faithfulness' or 'truthfulness', the name could carry the author's irony and be designed to point up the faithlessness of Israel with which he is so concerned. Alternatively, it may be that there were other stories in circulation about the eighth-century prophet which were not included in Kings, but which would have explained the author's choice for us had they survived. In the end we cannot read the author's mind here, but we can take note of one or two features of the Kings narrative and make our own connections. Jeroboam II came late in the history of the northern kingdom. The hopes engendered by the expansion of the kingdom during his reign turned out to be false. His death sparked off a period of intrigue and civil strife, and the year after it saw three kings on the throne in quick succession. Soon after the third of those died came the disaster of the first Assyrian invasion, and soon after that came the end of everything. In the narrative of Kings, Jonah ben Amittai is the last prophet we hear of in the kingdom of Israel before its fall. He is in that account, therefore, the last one in Israel to have had access to the mind of God, the one who might have brought the people back to him before it was too late.

Playing hide-and-seek with God

The story of Jonah begins in a conventional enough way, not with the call of the prophet, but with his commissioning. 'Now the word of the Lord came to Jonah the son of Amittai, saying, "Arise, go . . ." ' The beginnings of the books of Hosea and Zechariah are similar, and commissioning stories are common in the Old Testament. The abrupt 'Arise, go' reminds us of Genesis 12, and more closely still of Elijah, sent by divine decree to Zarephath, and later to Naboth's vineyard in Jezreel (see 1 Kings 17.9, which has the exact 'Arise, go', and 21.18 – 'Arise, go down').

But once we are beyond the word 'go' we are in unknown territory. 'Arise, go to Nineveh, that great city, and cry against it; for their evil has come up before me.' Other prophets had felt called to pronounce God's judgement on foreign nations, and in particular upon Israel's enemies. Nahum, as we have seen, declared the death sentence upon Nineveh itself. Moses had been commissioned to beard the Pharaoh of Israel's slavery and opression in his den. But none had been asked to go to 'Berlin'. None had been asked before to take the anger of God into 'Hitler's bunker'. Jonah is here being asked the impossible, and for this reason surely we cannot be surprised when, though he does 'arise', he promply turns and runs. Did not Isaiah at his call protest that he could not speak the word of God, for he was 'a man of unclean lips' (Isa.6.5)? Did not Jeremiah at his call cry, 'Ah, Lord God! Behold, I do not know how to speak, for I am only a youth' (Jer. 1.6)? And the great Moses, given at the Burning Bush the task closest to Jonah's, himself protested, 'Who am I that I should go to Pharaoh, and bring the sons of Israel out of Egypt?' (Exod. 3.11), and went on protesting (4.1,10) until at last in desperation he begged God to send someone else, and succeeded for a moment in exhausting the divine patience (4.13–14).

Yet both Isaiah and Jeremiah quickly relented, and for years courageously spoke the word of God, and Moses went to Pharaoh, and went again and again, until he brought the sons of Israel out of Egypt. Jonah, asked to do the impossible, in fact does the impossible: he turns and runs. Commanded by the word of God to go east by land, he takes ship and goes by sea as far west as he possibly can (Tarshish in this story probably represents the furthest point west that a Jew could think of; it is a kind of occidental Timbuktu).

Jonah does the impossible in another sense, too: he sails 'away from the presence of the Lord'. The sacred songs of his people celebrated God as creator and lord of all the earth. In particular they proclaimed him master of the sea, the one who at creation 'gathered the waters of the sea as in a bottle' (Ps. 33.7), and who brought his people out of slavery in Egypt by dividing a sea in half: 'Thy way was through the sea, thy path through the great waters' (Ps.77.19). He was the God who, when men 'went down to the sea in ships . . . commanded, and raised the stormy wind, which lifted up the waves of the sea', so that ' . . . they reeled and staggered like drunken men, and were at their wits' end', who then 'made the storm be still, and the waves of the sea were hushed' (Ps.107. 23, 25, 27, and 29). Another psalm had these words:

> Whither shall I go from thy Spirit?
>   Or whither shall I flee from thy presence?
> If I ascend to heaven, thou art there!
>   If I make my bed in Sheol, thou art there!
> If I take the wings of the morning
>   and dwell in the uttermost parts of the sea,
> even there thy hand shall lead me,
>   and thy right hand shall hold me.   (139.7–10)

Jonah is a fool, a buffoon, and he only underlines the absurdity of his flight by hiding in the dark recesses of the bottom of the boat, as if he hopes his God might not be able to spot him there. He underlines it again by his pompous answer to the captain, 'I am a Hebrew; and I fear the Lord, the God of heaven, *who made the sea and the dry land*'!

He can hardly be surprised when God hurls a great wind upon the sea, and brings a mighty storm, so that in the Hebrew we hear the waves crashing against the sides of the boat – the two words of verse 4 translated 'threatened to break up' are '*hishshebah lehishshaber*'. And yet he will not face the truth. He goes down to the bottom of the boat, and sinks into the sleep whose depths bring oblivion and border upon death. When exactly he does this is not clear. Hebrew has only one past tense, so that the pluperfects of our versions of the second half of verse 5 could just as easily be translated as aorists: 'But Jonah *went* down . . . and *lay* down, and *fell* into a deep sleep.' In other words we could see him, and I suspect we are meant to see him, as deliberately turning his back on God's storm, just as at the start he turned his back on his word.

However we settle the ambiguity of the Hebrew, it is plain that

Jonah, the Israelite, the prophet of God, does not compare well with the pagan sailors. They do not turn away to oblivion, they do not play hide-and-seek with the forces of heaven. They face the storm, and feel its terror. They turn at once to their gods, and when their prayers seem to go unheeded, and their efforts to lighten the ship do nothing to diminish the danger, the captain is quick to find Jonah and bid him pray also. His 'What do you mean?' is in the Hebrew the same as God's 'What are you doing?' in that question put to Elijah on Sinai/Horeb, 'What are you doing here, Elijah?'. His 'Arise, call upon your god!' recalls Jonah's commission, 'Arise, go to Nineveh . . . and cry against it', especially when we realize that the same Hebrew word is behind 'cry' and 'call'. The captain unwittingly echoes the words of God, and reminds Jonah of his God-given task. But he gets no response from Jonah at all.

So, while Jonah remains with his face turned to the wall, the sailors try another ploy. Knowing this is no ordinary storm, but the hurl of divine anger, they cast lots to gain access to the minds of the gods. Their methods are unerring. The lot falls, as it must, on Jonah. But they do not cast their accusations at him. Instead they seek him out as the one who can explain their plight. They do not say to him, as the prophet Nathan said to the guilty king David, 'You are the man' (2 Sam. 12.7), but instead they ask him to tell them 'on whose account this evil has come upon' them. Like their captain they echo Jonah's commission with that word 'evil'. But their request, so remarkably free from rebuke, and their urgent questioning meet only with Jonah's absurd self-importance: 'I am a Hebrew; and I fear the Lord, the God of heaven, who made the sea and the dry land.' His words do not begin to answer all their questions, and yet they are enough to reveal to them what is going on, and overwhelm their minds with a fear greater than that brought by the storm. They know now that Jonah is attempting the impossible. They know he is trying to escape from the presence of God, and they understand the full horror of his flight. 'What is this that you have done?' is now their cry. They understand now that whether they are saved from the storm or not depends on Jonah. 'What shall we do to you?' they ask him. For the first time Jonah shares their insight. 'Take me up,' he says, 'and hurl me into the sea; then the sea will quiet down for you; for I know it is because of me that this great tempest has come upon you.'

At last, so it might appear, Jonah has ceased to think only of himself. Yet the storyteller leaves Jonah's motives unstated. He leaves us free to see his plea as a moment of heroic self-sacrifice, unmatched by anything he says or does anywhere else in the story. But he allows us also to read it as an attempt to escape from God once and for all. The ancient Israelites did not develop a belief in life with God after death until some time after the book of Jonah was written. Instead, despite those verses of Psalm 139 we have already quoted, they pictured Sheol, the place where the dead led their shadowy existence, as beyond the reach of God and beyond any hope of communication with him (see Isa. 38.18, for example, or Pss. 88.12 and 115.17). Well might we see Jonah's request to be thrown into the sea as his next step in the search for oblivion, as his last desperate ploy in his game of hide-and-seek with God, his last attempt (or nearly so; he will, in fact, make one more) to rid himself of the horror of his mission to Nineveh.

Certainly the more negative of the two interpretations appears to be the one adopted by the sailors. Though the storm grows fiercer and fiercer, they try to row for the shore. Back on dry land Jonah will be able to fulfil his mission. Yet still they are thwarted by God's storm, and in the end they are left with no alternative, but to do as Jonah says. But before they throw him overboard, they pray, no longer each to his own god, but to Jonah's Yahweh, 'the God of heaven, who made the sea and the dry land'. Their prayer does not rebuke God for catching them up in his anger with Jonah. Still their words contain no hint of accusation. Like their captain with his 'perhaps the god will give a thought to us', they acknowledge God's freedom to act as he will. '. . . for thou, O Lord, hast done as it pleased thee' is all they have to say about the storm. Their prayer is chiefly concerned with a plea that God should not hold Jonah's death against them, and find them guilty of murder. Their words show a quick appreciation of the horror felt by the Israelites and their God at the shedding of innocent blood (see Deut. 21.1–9, Jer. 26.12–15). Jonah, once more by contrast, seems not to have thought of the predicament in which his death might place them.

When Jonah is cast into the sea, the storm at once subsides. It is as if God has been appeased by human sacrifice, and the sailors, coming from theological worlds where such things were well understood, are overcome once more by a great 'fear'. But this fear is no longer terror. It is the reverence and awe of those who have encountered Yahweh in all his power. It is the 'fear of the Lord' which the sages of the book of Proverbs claimed to be 'the beginning of wisdom' (Prov. 1.7; 9.10). Together with their prayer to him, it marks their beginnings as worshippers of Yahweh. They will need to learn a more sophisticated theology. They will need to be taught the horror with which the Israelites and their God regarded human sacrifice, but that can wait. For the moment it is enough that they sacrifice an animal to him, like Noah after the Flood, and make vows.

Their deliverance is complete. They are saved from the storm, and to use the terms of the ancient Israelites, from the vanity of their idolatry. At every turn Jonah has been shown up for who he is by their courage, their selflessness, their wisdom, and by their piety and faith. And yet in trying to turn his back on his life, his God, and his mission, he has ended up being instrumental in their conversion. Such is the irony of this first chapter, and such, we might add, is the mischief of God, whose twinkle in the eye enables good to come where there seems no hope of it at all.

Jonah is a fool, a buffoon, and he will go on playing the part with a will in this story. But we do well to pause, now that we have reached the end of the first scene, and reflect upon his foolishness. The folly of the man and the woman in the Garden was far too close to home for our comfort. Perhaps Jonah's folly is also. His refusal to face the truth he knows, the truth, that is, of the nature of God and his terrible demands, his preoccupation with himself, his self-importance, even his preferring oblivion to reality, no doubt were designed by the storyteller to put his original audience to shame. We need to ask whether they put us to shame any the less.

A ridiculous psalm of thanksgiving

The Hebrew text and the Jerusalem Bible place the chapter division after 1.16. There can be no doubt they are right. The second scene of the story opens with the coming of the fish, not with Jonah's psalm from its belly, though we need the psalm to fill in the details of what happens.

The sailors were wrong in thinking of Jonah as God's sacrifice, if that indeed is what they supposed. In his psalm Jonah gives us a graphic account of his descent in the sea, and it is plain that he comes within a hair's breadth of dying. He sinks beneath the surface and falls down, down, till he is too deep for even the roots of the mountains, and the seaweed begins to weave his funeral shroud about his head. The ancient Israelites sometimes pictured the land as floating on a vast mass of water. That is what the writer is doing here, and we are asked to imagine Jonah looking up through the strands of weed clinging to his face at the underside of the mountains receding above him. Still he goes down, until he is in the land of the dead, in the very 'belly of Sheol', as he describes it. But just as the bars of death's gates are about to be slammed tight shut upon him, God's fish suddenly appears and snatches him away. The fish, if we use Jonah's other metaphor, has had to swim right down death's throat to get him.

The poem is on one level a brilliant description of a drowning man. But it is also a psalm of thanksgiving that represents one of the high points in Old Testament comic writing. Scholars used to think that the storyteller, or even a later editor, had taken the psalm from another source and inserted it in the text. But recent work has tended to emphasize the strong links between it and the rest of the story, and we might add the observation that if the storyteller or his editor did not write it, then they were most extraordinarily fortunate to find something which fitted so well, and which at the same time fitted so ill! For coming at this stage of the story it is at once singularly appropriate and marvellously out of place. Like much comic writing, it is a blend of the congruous and the incongruous.

At the time he sings it Jonah has, it is true, been rescued from death, and has quite unexpectedly been given back his life to live. To sing a psalm of thanksgiving for deliverance is, on that reckoning, the proper thing to do. Just as the sailors were quick to perceive the divine origins of the storm, so Jonah has at once realized the identity of the one who has engineered his rescue. For the first time in the story he turns towards his God, and not away from him, and in the cry which closes his psalm, 'Deliverance belongs to the Lord!' he speaks one of the great truths with which the story is concerned.

All this is in place. But if we still think that it is absurd to hear such beautifully phrased gratitude coming from the belly of a fish, then, of course, we are right. There were stories enough in the ancient world of people, even an entire ship's crew, being swallowed by fish and coming out unscathed, and several modern fairy stories have the same motif: Pinocchio and Geppetto escape from a shark, and Little Red Riding Hood's grandma, the duck in 'Peter and the Wolf', and the kids in 'The Wolf and the Seven Little Kids' all survive the stomachs of wolves. Even so we might be forgiven for thinking Jonah's psalm a little premature! He may be out of the frying-pan, but he is certainly not yet out of the fire. He is still, it would appear, having trouble facing the reality of his situation.

The psalm looks forward to the future, and makes clear that Jonah

has at least lost his despair and his longing for oblivion. Indeed he
forgets that it was at his own request that he was thrown into the sea,
and accuses God of nearly drowning him instead! But he has lost
nothing of his self-centredness or his pomposity, and he shows in the
belly of the fish a deviousness we have not seen before. Over and over
again in the poem the words 'I' and 'me' appear. He quotes songs
from the book of Psalms, but sometimes with subtle alternations of
the text that put him at the centre of things. 'Then I said, "I am cast
out from thy presence; yet I shall look again upon thy holy temple" '
(the RSV mistranslates here) replaces Psalm 31's 'As for me, I said in
my haste, "I am cut off from thy presence. But thou didst hear my
supplications, when I cried to thee for help" ' (Ps. 31. 22). Psalm
120's 'To the Lord in my distress I called, and he answered me' (a
translation of verse 1 that indicates the word order of the Hebrew
more successfully than the RSV does) becomes in the mouth of
Jonah, 'I called out of my distress to the Lord, and he answered me.'
His psalm lacks the humility of genuine thanksgiving, and indeed,
rather than giving evidence of his belated submission to God, it
reveals that he now has his own plans for the future. Twice he refers
to the temple, and he promises that he will complete his act of
thanksgiving there in the proper manner. But God does not wish to
see Jonah in Jerusalem. God wants Jonah in Nineveh, and of that
place, or of the commission that sent Jonah running, the psalm
makes no mention. Nowhere in all its fine lines is there a hint of
remorse or repentance.

The talk of sacrifice and vows near the end of the poem reminds
us, of course, of the sailors after the end of the storm. Once more the
storyteller-poet would have us compare his hero with those pagan
converts, and remember how he fared in the comparison. With yet
more, almost bitter irony he makes quite sure the point is not lost on
us. For Jonah's pledge follows immediately upon a claim that 'Those
who pay regard to vain idols forsake the mercy that could be theirs.'
Even when we acknowledge that these words represent a deliberate
toning down of Psalm 31's 'I hate those who pay regard to vain idols'
(v.6: only there and in Jonah 2.8 does a particular form of the
Hebrew verb translated 'pay regard' occur), we can scarcely believe
our ears. After the events of the storm scene, the qualities revealed in
the pagan sailors and their captain, and their attempts to save Jonah
and rescue the purposes of God, nothing in the psalm is further out
of place than this, nothing speaks louder of blind prejudice and
arrogance. The ensuing 'Deliverance belongs to the Lord!' has in

this prophet's mouth a hollow ring about it. God will have to teach him what the words mean.

The impossible happens

God's first lesson is given immediately. In the most undignified manner Jonah is delivered from the fish. Thereby God would prick his pomposity and remind him of reality. But the deeper meaning of deliverance for Jonah himself is not conveyed by the fish vomiting him up on the shore, but by God repeating his original commission. If Jonah is to find deliverance from God, he must go to Nineveh. He will only begin to find his own salvation in obedience and all that obedience entails. In Nineveh he will discover what 'deliverance belongs to the Lord' means for his fellow human beings, and for the rest of God's creation, and if he can come to terms with that, then his own deliverance will be complete.

So the story begins all over again: 'Arise, go to Nineveh, that great city, and cry unto it . . .' (in the Hebrew the same three verbs occur in 3.2 as were used in 1.2). What exactly Jonah is to 'cry' is left unsaid. The Hebrew would suggest that God's message for the city is the same as it has been all along, but it was not clear from the terms of Jonah's first commission exactly what it was. The storyteller leaves it a mystery, and it will remain so to the end. We are not to presume that God is making an impossible task yet more difficult by not telling his prophet what to say. It is we, not Jonah, who are left in the dark. No doubt he is given full and clear instructions, as prophets were. But when we hear his proclamation in the city, we will be left wondering whether he is truly speaking the word of God, and has spoken all that God told him to say, or whether he is merely giving vent to his own prejudice and bitterness.

The storm, his long descent through the sea towards death, three days and nights in a fish's belly, and the indignity of his return to dry land, have at least taught Jonah that it is no use trying to run and hide from God. He goes to Nineveh 'according to the word of the Lord'. It was a journey of several hundred miles, for this 'Berlin' lay on the eastern side of the Tigris river, but the storyteller does not delay us with its details. We have, after all, waited long enough for Jonah to reach the city.

The description we are given of Nineveh is interesting. 'An exceedingly great city' is an attempt to translate a Hebrew phrase which means literally, 'a great city to God'. Among the poems of the anonymous prophet of the Babylonian exile known as Second Isaiah we find one celebrating the majesty of God the Creator. It describes God as

> . . . he who sits above the circle of the earth,
> and its inhabitants are like grasshoppers,

and it compares the nations to 'a drop from a bucket' and to 'the dust on the scales' (Isa. 40.22 and 15). But Jonah's Nineveh seems large even to God 'looking down' from heaven. It takes, we are told, three days to cross. If we had the pagan world in miniature on board ship, we now have it writ very large indeed.

The historical Nineveh was nothing like so big, of course. The story gives us a vast metropolis, as large as the very largest cities of the modern world. In fact, until as late as the early years of the seventh century BCE Nineveh covered no more than 180 acres. When king Sennacherib then turned it into the capital of his empire and greatly enlarged it, its new walls still only enclosed a thousand acres. But in the book of Jonah we are not dealing with precise historical records, but with storytelling whose precision is just as real, but of a different kind. What we need to ask is why the writer should describe Nineveh in the way he does. The answers (for there are more than one) are not hard to find, and they will emerge as we proceed.

Jonah reaches Nineveh, but he does not go much further. Though he goes a day's journey beyond the gates, he does no more than 'begin' to go into the city, so vast is its extent. Not yet at the dark centres of power, he proclaims his message, 'Yet forty days, and Nineveh will be overthrown!' That is all. He has gone all that way for what in the Hebrew is just five words. He provides no reason for the coming catastrophe. He says nothing of the stench of evil which reached the nostrils of his God and prompted his commissioning. He makes no call to repentance. His words contain no hint of mercy or pity, no suggestion of any hope for the future. They do not even make clear to the Ninevites whose words they are, for they lack the 'Thus says the Lord' that Israelite prophets used to introduce their oracles. They speak only of inescapable destruction, in terms that remind us of the devastation of Sodom and Gomorrah (see Gen. 19. 25, 29). As we have already said, we are left wondering whether Jonah has fulfilled God's mission, or his own.

But the Ninevites do not hesitate. Jonah's ugly words bring them at once to belief in God, to spontaneous acknowledgement of their wickedness, and to hope of salvation. The entire population of this huge metropolis proclaims a fast and puts on sackcloth. When their king gets to hear of it, he goes to even greater lengths. He lays aside all the trappings of his terrifying power, clothes his own body with sackcloth, and exchanges his throne for a pile of ashes. He issues a decree which sets the official seal on the people's fast, and underlines its severity. But it does much more than that. Assyrian annals, in their records of the capture or surrender of enemy cities, frequently refer to their populations in terms not only of men, women and children, but of domestic animals also. We saw ourselves in chapter 4 that oxen, sheep, and asses were listed among those slaughtered by the Israelites at Jericho. So now the king and the nobles of Nineveh make sure that every living thing in the city takes up the fast and is clad in the garb of mourning and penitence, and uses its strength to cry to God. Furthermore they turn the ritual into a great act of repentance. They recognize that they and their people are no better than the generation whose 'evil' and 'violence' provoked the Flood (see Gen. 6.5, 11, 13), and in great shame they put aside all the arrogance, all the brutality, all the ruthless seeking after and clinging to power for which they were so famed. In the middle of the storm in chapter 1 the ship's captain tried to rouse Jonah from his oblivion with the words, 'Arise, call upon your god! Perhaps the god will give a thought to us, so that we do not perish.' Now in Nineveh the end of the royal decree echoes those words: 'Who knows, God may yet repent and turn from his fierce anger, so that we do not perish?' Behind the uncompromising harshness of Jonah's proclamation, these ancient 'Nazis' catch a glimpse of the mercy of God, and of his freedom to show it even in the most unexpected places. Like the sea-captain, they make no attempt to force God's hand, they do not presume anything. They know the fate that justice demands of them, but having turned to God, they will wait and see if he will turn to them.

It is all too good to be true, of course. We have come across the theatre of the absurd in the Old Testament already. Now we have found it again. The picture created is ridiculous. The absurdity of such a people as the Assyrians turning to God in so whole-hearted and instant a fashion is transparent. The historical Nineveh stopped terrorizing the rest of the Ancient Near East not because of its conversion, but because it was conquered by the Babylonians. The storyteller seems to go out of his way to underline how ridiculous it all is by having the animals join in the ritual, even in the crying mightily to God. We know from the book of Judith in the Apocrypha that people might put sackcloth on their animals at a time of acute national crisis (Judith 4.10), but the animals of Nineveh are bidden to go to lengths that are quite implausible.

Yet God takes their act of repentance wholly seriously. These absurd Ninevites and their ridiculous animals turn God's heart. At the making of the Golden Calf at Sinai God cried in his anger to Moses, 'I have seen this people, and behold, it is a stiff-necked people; now therefore let me alone, that my wrath may burn hot against them and I may consume them' (Exod. 32.9–10). Yet when Moses then pleaded with him, at once '. . . the Lord repented of the evil which he said he would do to his people' (32.14). The writer of Jonah quotes Exodus 32.14 very nearly word for word: 'When God saw what they did, how they turned from their evil way, *God repented of the evil which he said he would do to them*; and he did not do it.' Thus he encouraged his original Jewish audience to recall how their own ancestors had driven God to distraction, and then had met with his astonishing mercy. Thus he invited them to compare themselves with the hated Assyrians, and to ask whether they had been any more deserving of God's forgiveness and compassion. According to his own implications, they could find the answer to that question also in Exodus 32. Whereas the Ninevites of his story turn away God's anger by a quite remarkable act of repentance, the Israelites at Sinai only survived because of the prompt and powerful pleading of the great Moses.

Accepting the pity of God

Were the story of Jonah to have ended there, with the great climax of Nineveh's repentance and God's own turning, then it would have risked not being taken seriously. The conversion of the Assyrians would have remained easy to laugh out of court, and the lessons set by the introduction of those words from Exodus could well have been dismissed as far too difficult to learn. The forgiveness of this God might have been quickly discounted as every bit as absurd as the Ninevites and their animals.

But, of course, the story does not end there. We have a whole scene still to come, and indeed the structure of the book might lead us to expect it to be the most important of all. We have had cause to notice already that storytellers tend to work in threes. The first two sections of the story of Jonah are complete. Twice he has been commissioned. The first time he disobeys and encounters storm, drowning, and the stomach of a fish. The second time he obeys, at least in part, and meets with the conversion of a city and his God. Now the third and final phase of the story begins, and the other stories suggest that here the pattern will be altered, and that this will be the place where the story 'happens'. Certainly by the time the storyteller is done, it will be hard to avoid taking him seriously.

The third section does not start with God's commission. In his ungracious way Jonah has, in a sense at least, already fulfilled that. But just as the story opened with God's anger, so this scene begins with the fury of his prophet.

The reaction of the Ninevites to Jonah's preaching was instantaneous. God himself responded at once to their repentance. Jonah now turns immediately to anger and bitter complaint. At the start God was angered, as well he might be, by the evil of the Ninevites. Now Jonah is enraged by God's forgiveness. His anger is meant to shock, and the Hebrew text makes that abundantly clear. For the term it uses for his 'displeasure' is, in fact, the word for 'evil' that God used of Nineveh, which the sailors employed to describe their plight in the midst of the storm, and which reappeared in the decree of the king of Nineveh and his nobles, and in the account of God's change of heart. The opening words of this scene could conceivably be translated, 'But it was, to Jonah, a great evil', or, 'But a great evil came upon Jonah.' The first of these translations would suggest that Jonah regards God's forgiveness as evil, the second that his anger is evil. We do not have to choose, indeed we must not choose between them, or even decide between 'evil' and 'displeasure'. The ambiguity is there, and is not to be ignored.

In the storm the sailors prayed. Jonah prayed from the stomach of the fish. Faced with the destruction of the city, the king and the nobles of Nineveh commanded the people and animals to pray. To underline the desperate nature of his plight now that God has forgiven, Jonah turns again to prayer. At last, or so it would seem, he explains why initially he turned and ran. 'That is why I made haste to flee to Tarshish; for I knew that thou art a gracious God and merciful, slow to anger, and abounding in steadfast love, and repentest of evil.' Whether we believe him is left up to us. It may be that we decide he is attempting to rationalize his actions in the light of what has taken place. It may be that we remain of the opinion that he fled because he was terrified of going to such a place as Nineveh. If we do, it is not then necessary for us to accuse him of deliberately lying to God, though, of course, he may be. The human facility for self-deception and for inventing the past is familiar enough.

Whether he speaks the truth or not, Jonah is trying to justify himself. Yet see how he does it! For the second time in this story, if not the third, he jumps from the frying-pan into the fire. He condemns himself with his own defence.

He describes God in words that would, for the most part, have been extremely familiar to those who first heard the story. They occur for the first time in the Old Testament, all but the last clause, in Exodus 34.6, on the lips of Moses soon after the incident of the Golden Calf, and are repeated or echoed in many other places in the literature, both early and late. They formed for the Israelites the most satisfactory summary of the nature of their God. In Jonah's mouth, as the burden of his defence, they take on a peculiar irony. The divine grace and mercy of which they speak only remind us of how little grace or mercy we have seen in Jonah. God's 'slowness to anger' underlines how quick to anger his prophet has been. His 'steadfast love', clear enough already in his patience with Jonah, and about to become clearer still, only makes us realize how little love there is about the prophet, and will make us smile even more broadly when soon we find him so fickle.

The words of Exodus 34 do more than sit in judgement on the one who speaks them. They make it clear that the reaction of God to the repentance of the Ninevites was quite typical of him. Jonah is right in a sense, just as he was right in what he said about God to the crew of the ship. Had he really foreseen that the Assyrians would repent, then indeed, by the insights of his own tradition he could have expected God to show them mercy, and to 'repent of evil' just as he did after the Golden Calf.

But Jonah's prayer is not yet finished: 'Therefore now, O Lord, take my life from me, I beseech thee, for it is better for me to die than to live.' Right at the start of the story we were given through God's 'Arise, go' a reminder of Elijah. This final scene is crowded with echoes of Elijah, and in particular of his journey to Sinai/Horeb. Jonah's plea to God to let him die is the first of them (see 1 Kings 19.4). The comparison with the great prophet of the ninth century introduces yet more irony. Elijah was driven to despair by the ruthlessness of Jezebel. Jonah is driven to precisely the same despair by the forgiveness of God.

When we explored the story of 1 Kings 19, we noticed how clearly

Elijah's journey mimicked the wanderings of the Israelites after the exodus from Egypt. So too Jonah's bitter complaint recalls the complaints of the Israelites in the desert (see Num. 14.2, also Exod. 16.3 and Num. 20.3). But while their complaints were mostly prompted by desperate thirst, starvation, or threat of slaughter, Jonah's stems from the giving of life to Nineveh. There remains, however, one source common to the complaints of the people and the prophet, namely insecurity. The Israelites craved in the desert for the security of their old life of slavery in Egypt. Jonah would rather die than leave the haven of his prejudice and hatred, and the security, too, no doubt, of his belief in God's justice. Some of his sacred traditions, particularly parts of Deuteronomy, Judges and Kings, as well as some of the songs in the book of Psalms, would have encouraged him towards a mechanical view of the justice of God, and the belief that righteousness was always rewarded by prosperity, and wickedness by disaster. Such thinking is still popular with many Christians, of course. But it leaves no room for the kind of mercy that Jonah encountered at Nineveh. That kind of mercy turns the world of mechanical justice upside down. That kind of mercy bursts wineskins. It makes life and God himself much more unpredictable. It can be more disturbing, more shocking, even, than God's anger, for that can always be readily explained. Jonah's despair, which seems at first so ridiculous and reprehensible, is eminently understandable. Once again we find this story cuts closer to the bone than we would care to admit.

God, in his great understanding, does not scold or condemn. As he did with Elijah, he asks Jonah a question, and like that put to Elijah, it is one of devastating simplicity: 'Do you do well to be angry?' When God asked 'What are you doing here, Elijah', Elijah answered him at length, in forceful terms. Jonah makes no reply, but turns on his heel, goes a little way off, makes a shelter for himself, and waits to see what will happen to the city.

His actions speak louder than words. No speech of his could have conveyed with such force his refusal to face the reality of God's forgiveness. He knew when he took the ship to Tarshish that he could not escape from God, but that did not stop him trying. Now he knows that God has 'repented of the evil which he had said he would do to them', but he will not accept it. Clinging to his old hatred and his old belief, he waits for Nineveh's forty days to be up. He is, of course, a buffoon, but a buffoon who still is perfectly understandable.

Yet there is something sinister, also, about his stand, just as there may well have been about Elijah's flight to Sinai/Horeb. This Jonah pits his will against the will of God, and throws his ugly prophecy into the ring with God's mercy. If Elijah may have wished to change the course of God's history, then Jonah would strive to usurp God's throne.

In God's response we have another example of his mischief. When Jonah was cast into the sea, God 'appointed' a fish to deliver him from drowning. Now he 'appoints' a gourd plant to grow and save him from the fierce heat of the sun (no doubt his own shelter is not all it might be!), and makes him like Elijah sitting underneath his broom tree (1 Kings 19.4). Soon he will 'appoint' a worm and a scorching wind, also.

Jonah is overjoyed! A plant and a little shade put all his world to rights! But next morning early God's worm gets to work, and in no time at all the plant is gone and the shade with it. To make matters worse a scorching wind begins at God's command to blow from the desert, and as the worm 'attacked' the gourd, so the wind 'attacks' Jonah's head (the two verbs are the same in the Hebrew). Immediately he resumes his search for oblivion, and he 'asks that he might die' (yet another echo of 1 Kings 19: the clause in the Hebrew is an idiomatic one, and occurs only here and in 1 Kings 19.4). 'It is better for me to die than to live,' he says. From the depths of despair to the dizzy heights of joy and down to the depths again, and all in the space of twenty-four hours! Such is the fickleness of this prophet, and no doubt the storyteller wished the hearers of his story to reflect amidst their laughter upon the fickleness of their own people, so shockingly exemplified by the generation of the exodus.

God's reply contains the last reminder of 1 Kings 19. When he made the gourd grow, he did not merely wish to give Jonah shade from the sun. He wished to save him from his 'evil'. (Once more in the Hebrew that word appears.) Through a little 'act of salvation' all his own, God tried to help him come to terms with the larger salvation of the city of Nineveh. But though the plant did bring joy, it was only joy at the drop in temperature. Jonah remained locked within his little world, shut up within his 'evil'. So now God must ask him again, 'Do you do well to be angry for the plant?' The echo of the twice repeated question at Sinai/Horeb is sharp and clear, but there is a difference too. The second question put to Elijah was exactly the same as the first. God's second question to Jonah has the addition of the words 'for the plant'. Nineveh for the moment seems forgotten. The matter concerns just God, and Jonah, and his own comfort. God squeezes into Jonah's world, and confronts him there, face to face. Jonah's response contains no reminder of Nineveh, and in it he reaches the height of his defiance of God and his purposes of redemption: 'I do well to be angry, angry enough to die.'

The story of Jonah is a tale of one extraordinary thing after another. Perhaps the most extraordinary of all now follows and closes the book: God asks Jonah another question. One might very well have expected him to turn on his own heel and go away, putting behind him this prophet who has tried his patience so much more in the end than the pagans of his world, so much more than the Assyrians and their king. But he refuses to leave. His dogged persistence is what the Israelites called 'steadfast love'. Ironically, Jonah has himself already declared it typical of him.

He begins by gently chiding Jonah, flattering him somewhat in the process. 'You pity the plant, for which you did not labour, nor did you make it grow, which came into being in a night, and perished in a night. And should I not pity Nineveh, that great city, in which there are more than a hundred and twenty thousand persons who do not know their right hand from their left, and also much cattle?' Of course, in truth Jonah has no pity for the plant. He feels sorry only for himself. God imputes better feelings to him than in fact he has, to soothe his anger with a little flattery, and at the same time to shame him all the more. In his own narrow world Jonah *ought* to be feeling sorry for the plant so soon destroyed by the worm. In God's much larger world he ought to share God's compassion for the people and animals of Nineveh.

With God's question the book comes to an end. We are not told Jonah's response. We are left free to imagine that perhaps he emerges from his booth the same man as he was when he turned and took ship for Tarshish. But he cannot leave the question unanswered. Even if he says nothing, his actions will still speak louder than words.

The first hearers of the story could not have left the question unanswered either. By closing his book so abruptly with it, the storyteller turned the question towards them, and demanded their answer. They who, through God's great gift of the torah, did know their right hand from their left, who knew and felt what the Assyrians had done to their people, who had been taught that their God was gracious and merciful, slow to anger and abounding in steadfast love, had to face the question of *the boundaries they put around his mercy*. They had to come to terms with the fact that those boundaries were of their own devising. They had to accept the freedom of God's forgiveness and compassion to go even into the very darkest places in his world, for surely if they went to Nineveh, their 'Berlin', then they might go anywhere.

But *we* are now the readers of Jonah. God's question is just as unerringly aimed at us. In a world and a church so adept in so many ways at hemming in the mercy of God, it should make us mighty uneasy and bring us to our knees.

God's words give rise to one more question that the book of Jonah teasingly does not answer. Did God save the Ninevites from destruction because of their repentance, or out of his sheer compassion? The answer seemed clear enough at the end of chapter 3, but now at the end of the book there is no mention of repentance, only of pity, no mention of what the Ninevites did, only of the feelings of God's heart.

Now, perhaps, it is clear why we said at the beginning of this chapter that Jonah would take us to the foot of the Cross.

SUGGESTIONS FOR FURTHER READING

The following books range widely over all or some of the texts covered in this book, and beyond them:

Robert Alter and Frank Kermode, eds, *The Literary Guide to the Bible*. London, Collins, 1987.

Robert Alter, *The Art of Biblical Narrative*. London, George Allen and Unwin, 1981.

Edwin M. Good, *Irony in the Old Testament*. 2nd ed., Sheffield, Almond Press, 1981.

Walter Brueggemann, *The Land: Place as Gift, Promise and Challenge in Biblical Faith*. Philadelphia, Fortress Press, 1977.

Phyllis Trible, *Texts of Terror: Literary-Feminist Readings of Biblical Narratives*. Philadelphia, Fortress Press, 1984.

The books below cover more specific areas of the texts dealt with in this book (and one of them is concerned with important narratives which we have neglected):

Anthony Phillips, *Lower than the Angels: Questions raised by Genesis 1–11*. London, BRF, 1983.

Michael Walzer, *Exodus and Revolution*. New York, Basic Books, 1985.

Terence E. Fretheim, *Deuteronomic History*. Nashville, Abingdon Press, 1983.

Walter Brueggemann, *David's Truth in Israel's Imagination and Memory*. Philadelphia, Fortress Press, 1985. An excellent book to read if you wish to explore the David stories.

Terence E. Fretheim, *The Message of Jonah*. Nashville, Abingdon Press, 1983.

Bruce Vawter, *Job and Jonah: Questioning the Hidden God*. New York, Paulist Press, 1985.

The St Andrew Press in Edinburgh produced in the 1980s a series of relatively brief and simple commentaries on the books of the Old Testament. They include the following:

Genesis 1–11, John C.L. Gibson, 1981
Genesis 12–50, John C.L. Gibson, 1982
Exodus, H.L. Ellison, 1982
Numbers, Walter Riggans, 1983
Joshua, Judges, and Ruth, A. Graeme Auld, 1984
Samuel, D.F. Payne, 1982
Kings, A. Graeme Auld, 1986
The Twelve Prophets, vol 1, Peter C. Craigie, 1984 (this includes Jonah)

INDEX OF BIBLICAL REFERENCES

INDEX OF NAMES AND SUBJECTS